Teamship:

52 Inspirational Readings
for Leaders

ISBN: 1-4196-9851-6
ISBN-13: 9781419698514

Visit www.booksurge.com to order additional copies.

Endorsements

"Building a team, unlike building a house, never gets completed. John Cionca and Fred Prinzing offer spiritual tools to keep the process going."

> — John Ortberg,
> Pastor and Author,
> Menlo Park Presbyterian Church

"Weekly meetings become a daily 'grind,' devoid of the larger purpose they are designed for, and driven by detail rather than vision. *Teamship* is a tool to refresh, re-focus, and inspire. It'll stay on my desk, if only to grab as I go into a meeting where I need a quick picture of interactive inspiration. Thanks!"

> — John Crosby,
> Senior Pastor,
> Christ Presbyterian Church, Edina, MN

"A marvelous ministry toolkit integrating biblical authority into practical, powerful, bite-sized lessons which will realign, encourage and empower ministry teams."

> — Jay Bennett,
> Chief Executive Officer,
> The Twin Cities Christian Foundation

"*Teamship* is a must-have for new and current team leaders. Considering the challenges of leading a team, this devotional provides a steady stream of useful and motivating reflections to help keep both the leader and the team on track in their relationships and mission."

> — Andrea Buczynski,
> Vice President for Global Leadership Development,
> Campus Crusade for Christ

"Great coaches motivate their teams to play well. *Teamship* is an awesome collection of 'Spiritual' locker room speeches where God motivates His ministry teams to excel in service."

> — Paul Borden,
> Author of *Hit the Bullseye* and *Direct Hit*

"Written with the framework of a MBA curriculum and interlaced with practical Scriptural applications, this book provides a freshly-brewed perspective to start a budget-minded day with succinct lessons on leadership."

> — Timothy Chan,
> Senior Pastor,
> Gaithersburg Chinese Alliance Church

"A neat book for church leader teams to read and reflect on each chapter, each week for a year. A Team Devotional book is a great concept for building needed teamship and common understandings among a church's leaders."

> — Dave Travis,
> Managing Director,
> Leadership Network

Teamship:

52 Inspirational Readings for Leaders

John R. Cionca and Fred W. Prinzing

Dedication

To

George K. *Brushaber*
President, Bethel University
1982–2008

for a life of leadership excellence
as churchman, educator and journalist

Thanks for your Kingdom orientation,
visionary leadership and servant spirit

Well done, good and faithful servant!

Contents

Preface

THE BIBLE is a book about God and humanity. Its primary theme is redemption—God drawing people into a relationship with Himself through His Son, Jesus Christ.

As His creation, we can learn more about ourselves from theology than we can from psychology and sociology combined. This is not to discredit these disciplines, for they provide great insights. And in reality, all truth is God's truth.

But the Owner's manual for humanity, the Bible, records God's perspective on life. It is generously packed with principles and case studies for our well-being. In the words of the source book itself:

> *For everything that was written in the past was written to teach us, so that through the endurance taught in the scriptures and the encouragement they provide we might have hope.* (Romans 14:4).

Teamship is designed to enable leadership teams to look at some of these case studies for guidance in their work together. The subtitle of this work denotes its desire to be *inspirational*—a means of drawing you closer to the Master. The work also aspires to be a *coaching* tool—providing advice on relational ministry.

So at the beginning of your team meetings, take a few moments to read a portion of Scripture and the coaching thoughts that follow. Read the devotions in the order provided, or select a particular theme from the listing in the Contents. And use the group exercises to get to know one another better and to press further the thematic principle.

Our Lord exampled for us the value of service:

> *For even the Son of Man did not come to be served,*
> *but to serve, and to give his life a ransom for many.*
> (Mark 10:45)

So enjoy your service together as a ministry team, and enjoy this resource along your leadership journey.

God's best!

John R. Cionca
Fred W. Prinzing

Acknowledgements

SINCERE APPRECIATION is given to friends who have encouraged this project, made suggestions and provided resources to bring it into reality. We also want to acknowledge the invaluable assistance that Sara Norton and Gloria Metz have provided, from the transcribing of initial thoughts, through the multiple revisions, to the finalizing of this manuscript. Recognition is also due to Bethel University, and particularly to Dr. Leland Eliason, Provost of the Seminary, for providing a class act learning community for both students and faculty.

We also want to honor our life journey partners. This year John and Barbara will celebrate their 39th year of marriage, and Fred and Anita Prinzing their 54th year of marriage. In addition to serving as ministry partners with us, these remarkable women have made deep impact in the lives of others through their own ministries. Thanks for sharing your love for God with us these many years.

It is also necessary to acknowledge that because of their relevance to ministry teams, a few of the meditations in this work have been modified from the authors' previous writings. *God's Constancy* was adapted from *God is Immutable* appearing in *Decision Magazine*, January, 1990. *Only You* has been adapted from a letter by the same title in *Dear Pastor: Ministry Advice from Seasoned Pastors.* And *Diplomacy, Keeping the Big Picture,* and *Prayer,* have been adapted from *Search Counsel: A Devotional Coaching Guide for Call Committees.* You probably would enjoy a full reading of these works, if applicable to your ministry direction.

Finally, we remain overwhelmed through the years that the transcendent, sovereign God of the universe would want to call us His children, that He would send His only Son to die in our place, and would invite us into His harvest field of service. *Now to the King eternal, immortal, invisible, the only God, be honor and glory for ever and ever. Amen!*

John R. Cionca

JOHN R. CIONCA is the executive director of Ministry Transitions, Inc. He also holds the position of professor of ministry leadership at Bethel Seminary in St. Paul, Minnesota. Dr. Cionca has served in full-time capacities as a youth pastor, minister of discipleship and lead pastor. He has also ministered in many churches as an interim pastor and transitions coach. John has authored, co-authored and edited eight books, his most recent works being *Before You Move: A Guide to Making Transitions in Ministry* and *Dear Pastor: Ministry Advice from Seasoned Pastors.*

Fred W. Prinzing

FRED W. PRINZING lives in the Northwest where he is involved in a ministry of teaching, preaching and writing. Dr. Prinzing leads retreats and teaches overseas. He has served as interim pastor in 29 churches as well as pastored both rural and urban churches. Fred's writings include *Handling Church Tensions Creatively* and *Mixed Messages,* a book on interracial marriage, co-authored with his wife, Anita. Together Fred and John have also coauthored *Search Counsel: A Devotional Coaching Guide for Call Committees.*

Enthusiasm

For this reason I kneel before the Father, from whom every family in heaven and on earth derives its name. I pray that out of his glorious riches he may strengthen you with power through his Spirit in your inner being, so that Christ may dwell in your hearts through faith. And I pray that you, being rooted and established in love, may have power, together with all the Lord's people, to grasp how wide and long and high and deep is the love of Christ, and to know this love that surpasses knowledge—that you may be filled to the measure of all the fullness of God. Now to him who is able to do immeasurably more than all we ask or imagine, according to his power that is at work within us, to him be glory in the church and in Christ Jesus throughout all generations, for ever and ever! Amen.

— Ephesians 3:14-21

FOR A NUMBER OF YEARS my [John] daughter's basketball team wore practice shirts with the expression "Attitude is Everything" printed on the back. And while attitude really isn't everything, her team's enthusiasm for the game pushed its members beyond the other teams in their conference.

Lee Iacocca, former chairman of Ford Motors, and subsequently of Chrysler Motors, made this statement: "When it comes to making a place run, motivation is everything!" Again, is motivation everything? Not likely. But from his leadership perspective, it is enormously important.

Chuck Swindoll, pastor, writer and teacher, made the following observation: "I am convinced that success in life is only 10 percent what happens to me and 90 percent my attitude about it." When I ask others to suggest a percentage that they would give to the circumstances/attitude ratio, very few have assessed the attitude contribution at less than 75 percent. Is attitude everything? No. But is it hugely important? Definitely!

A survey of human resource managers revealed that 2,332 out of 2,756 respondents ranked enthusiasm as the first thing they sought during an applicant interview. Do they look for more? Of course. But note how important they believe enthusiasm is to job performance.

In another survey, when self-made millionaires were asked what contributed to their success, they responded: Ability–5 percent; Knowledge – 5 percent; Discipline – 10 percent; Attitude – 40 percent; and Enthusiasm – 40 percent.

Finally, let us remember what Henry Ford said: "You can do anything if you have enthusiasm. Enthusiasm is the yeast that makes your hopes rise to the stars. With it, there is accomplishment. Without it, there are only alibis."

Obviously, surgeons, professors and electricians all need requisite competencies for their professions. Discipline is also important to push oneself forward. But it's people's attitude and enthusiasm that distinguish them in their fields. Interview those who have received awards such as Colleague of the Month, Teacher of the Year or Lifetime Achievement, and you will feel the energetic enthusiasm these people have for their work.

Have you noticed how classrooms come alive, how Bible studies flourish, how community projects multiply and how lives are transformed when enthusiastic leaders draw us into their dreams? Their passions are contagious. And why not? Nothing is more energizing than helping people jump on God's bandwagon.

So take a moment and let these scriptures fuel your ministry enthusiasm:

- ♦ "You, dear children, are from God and have overcome them, because the One who is in you is greater than the one who is in the world" (1 John 4:4).

- ♦ "'For I know the plans I have for you,' declares the LORD, 'plans to prosper you and not to harm you, plans to give you hope and a future'" (Jeremiah 29:11).

- ♦ "And surely I am with you always, to the very end of the age" (Matthew 28:20b).

- ♦ "And we know that in all things God works for the good of those who love Him, who have been called according to His purpose" (Romans 8:28).

- ♦ "Now to Him who is able to do immeasurably more than all we ask or imagine, according to His power that is at work within us, to Him be glory in the church and in Christ Jesus throughout all generations, for ever and ever! Amen" (Ephesians 3:20, 21).

As leaders we have the high privilege of helping people know God better, and influencing them to embrace His values. This ministry to which God calls us is exciting. And God Himself is fully behind our service. So serve heartily with full enthusiasm!

Group Exercise:

Did you grow up in a mainly glass-half-full or glass-half-empty environment?

Who has been a positive influence in your life?

Team Prayer:

Dear God, from these scriptures we see that You are with us and are for us. We are overwhelmed by Your provision and Your presence in our lives. Lift our eyes to see how white the harvest truly is. May we never see the glass of life only half full. May we always see it overflowing with possibilities because You are life. Please charge us with a godly enthusiasm for the Kingdom work before us. Amen!

Final Thought:

I can do all this through Him,
who gives me strength.
—**Philippians 4:13**

The Withness Factor

The next day the rulers, the elders and the
teachers of the law met in Jerusalem. Annas the
high priest was there, and so were Caiaphas, John,
Alexander and others of the high priest's family.
They had Peter and John brought before them and
began to question them: 'By what power or what
name did you do this?' Then Peter, filled with the
Holy Spirit, said to them: 'Rulers and elders of
the people! If we are being called to account today
for an act of kindness shown to a man who was
lame and are being asked how he was healed,
then know this, you and all the people of Israel: It
is by the name of Jesus Christ of Nazareth, whom
you crucified but whom God raised from the dead,
that this man stands before you healed. Jesus
is 'the stone you builders rejected, which has
become the cornerstone.' Salvation is found in no
one else, for there is no other name given under
heaven by which we must be saved.' When they
saw the courage of Peter and John and realized

> that they were unschooled, ordinary men, they were astonished and they took note that these men had been with Jesus.

— Acts 4:5–13

ONE OF THE MOST SIGNIFICANT theological words in the Bible is the little word *with*. Although it's not a long word like propitiation or sanctification, it is critically important for personal transformation. We grow in our relationship to God when we spend time with Him. We also grow in our relationships to each other when we spend time with one another. Unfortunately, too many Christians let the pressures and pace of life keep them from developing quality relationships.

A number of years ago I [John] asked a group of young adults to recall a childhood experience that still affects them today. One young man responded: "When I was a child I remember asking my dad to play ball with me. He didn't have the time. I know my dad loves me, but I still remember that incident to this day, and wish he had taken just five minutes to show me some pointers. He never did. Ever!"

A second man recalled: "When I was a child, I always loved to watch Bugs Bunny on Saturday mornings. It was on fairly early, but my dad would wake up and come down and watch the show with me. For as long as I remember he did that with me. He never said much. He just smiled and laughed as I mimicked everything that the cartoons did. I loved Saturday mornings!"

Can you feel the disappointment in the first response versus the joy in the second? The difference in the experiences of these two men is the Withness Factor.

The power of being with another is seen clearly in the transformation of Peter and John. In the passage above, the Sanhedrin could not help but notice "that these men had been *with* Jesus" (v. 13).

So what keeps us from building a deeper relationship with God and others? What hinders us from knowing the blessings of friendship?

The first barrier to withness is a shortage of time. For many, the amount of work and activities that cry out for attention each day is overwhelming. Second, because we are trying so hard to keep all of our plates spinning, our self-focus hinders us from noticing when someone else's plate begins to wobble. Finally, a more challenging barrier to witness is that we may just not like the other person. Whether a coworker or family member, we avoid people who cause us pain.

But as Christians we can nurture withness in spite of these hindrances. Three focused practices can counteract them.

First, we can establish margin to gain time. "Be very careful, then, how you live—not as unwise but as wise, making the most of every opportunity" (Ephesians 5:17). We need to say no to some things, so that we can say yes to some people.

Second, we can become students of others. "Each of you should not only look to your own interests, but also the interests of others" (Philippians 2:4). Focused listening and careful observation enable us to see beyond our own needs and priorities.

And third, we can offer praise and exercise patience toward individuals we would rather avoid. "Be completely humble and gentle, be patient, bearing with one another in love" (Ephesians

4:2). When people feel better about themselves, they will be more cordial to others.

Group Exercise:

In pairs respond to the question:
With whom do you sense a need to spend more time right now? Why?

Take a moment to pray for one another.

Team Prayer:

Dear Lord, draw us even closer to You, so that we may better reflect Your heart. Remind us each day that You value people. Thanks for placing us together as a ministry team. May lives be touched because of Your presence with us and Your transforming love among us. Amen!

Final Thought:

When the very elements that make up this universe dissolve in fervent heat, only human beings will remain. Choose to love people rather than things.

— Larry Richards

Appreciation

Paul and Timothy, servants of Christ Jesus, to all God's holy people in Christ Jesus at Philippi, together with the overseers and deacons: Grace and peace to you from God our Father and the Lord Jesus Christ. I thank my God every time I remember you. In all my prayers for all of you, I always pray with joy because of your partnership in the gospel from the first day until now, being confident of this, that he who began a good work in you will carry it on to completion until the day of Christ Jesus. It is right for me to feel this way about all of you, since I have you in my heart and, whether I am in chains or defending and confirming the gospel, all of you share in God's grace with me. God can testify how I long for all of you with the affection of Christ Jesus. And this is my prayer: that your love may abound more and more in knowledge and depth of insight, so that you may be able to discern what is best and may be pure and blameless

*for the day of Christ, filled with the fruit of
righteousness that comes through Jesus Christ—
to the glory and praise of God.*
— Philippians 1:1–11

A HIGHLIGHT EACH YEAR FOR our [Fred's] church staff and their spouses was a two-day retreat at the Oregon Coast. It was primarily a time for relaxation and strengthening of relationships. Some people hiked, others played games, while the rest sat around eating junk food and talking.

Often our activities had to be adjusted because of the ever-present rain. One year a driving rainstorm limited our options to indoor activities. Someone suggested that we spend a couple of hours writing thank you notes to the church members. The idea was received with enthusiasm. As we read through the roster, various staff members volunteered to write a note to each individual or family listed. It was a joyful and satisfying experience as we reflected on the members of the body and their unique contribution to the church.

Our joy was minimal, however, compared to the response we received from church members the following Sunday. One man who had been a member for 40 years commented, "This is the first time I have ever received a thank you note from anyone in the congregation." How many people seldom, if ever, hear the words *thank you*?

The story is told of a man who decided to show his love and appreciation to his wife by giving her a bouquet of flowers even though it wasn't a special occasion. Holding the flowers behind him, he rang the doorbell. "Honey, I love you," he said when she opened the door. His wife, overwhelmed by this unexpected gesture, fainted. The man hurried into the house for a wet cloth and placed it on her forehead. As his wife regained her strength, she sat up and said: "Thank you." Then he fainted.

It's easy to forget to thank people for their contribution to ministry. The Apostle Paul knew that the believers at Philippi struggled with this problem. Therefore, he not only thanked God for their service, but he also expressed his appreciation to them directly.

If you are like most leaders, your ministry effectiveness is related to the efforts, prayers, finances and encouragement of others. So take time to express your gratitude to these people for what they mean to your ministry and to the overall mission of your organization.

As a praise exercise, make it a goal this week to thank at least three people for their presence and contribution. It may be especially edifying to express appreciation to those serving in other areas of ministry. In a church, for example, a youth leader could express appreciation to someone in the children's ministry, or a singles' volunteer might send a note of thanks to a member of the worship team. As this type of cross-functional valuing is expressed, the church will grow in strength and unity.

Group Exercise:

In a circle response, share with your teammates the name of one of the people to whom you will express appreciation this week.

What do you value about that person?

Team Prayer:

Gracious Father, thank You for being such a giving God. We are grateful for Your presence and Your many gifts. Please grant us one more thing— grateful hearts. We appreciate You for the many giving people You have brought into this ministry. Help us to take time to express our appreciation to them. Amen!

Final Thought:

Many a flower placed on a person's grave should have been given while the person was alive.

Purpose

They devoted themselves to the apostles' teaching
and to fellowship, to the breaking of bread and
to prayer. Everyone was filled with awe at the
many wonders and signs performed by the
apostles. All the believers were together and had
everything in common. They sold property and
possessions to give to anyone who had need.
Every day they continued to meet together in the
temple courts. They broke bread in their homes
and ate together with glad and sincere hearts,
praising God and enjoying the favor of all the
people. And the Lord added to their number daily
those who were being saved.

— Acts 2:42–47

HEALTHY CHURCHES AND EFFECTIVE TEAMS major on the
majors and minor on the minors. Ministries that get stuck
frequently fuss about particular methods or preferences. They
argue about programs, curriculum and schedules. They get

hung up on preferred forms, forgetting that forms are merely outlets to accomplish larger purposes.

As leaders we must help our people see the greater picture of ministry. We must continually remind them that Christ founded the Church for a purpose. Effective ministries always lift up the core disciple-making functions of quality teaching, comprehensive care-giving, dynamic worship and missional outreach.

Teaching is equipping people in biblical truth so that they will in turn teach others. Christ's commission to leaders includes "teaching them to observe everything I have commanded you" (Matthew 28:20). Since there are no end users in Christianity, we can never be satisfied with merely presenting lessons. We can only rejoice when our people mature to the point where they can help others in their understanding of Christ (see 2 Timothy 2:2).

Care giving is the flow of Christ's compassion from one believer to another. It is not primarily the job of a pastor or board. It's the entire body of Christ using its giftedness to minister to one another. Therefore, it is our responsibility as leaders to set up vehicles for relationship building. Some people will connect through study groups, some through support groups, and some through service teams. Guiding people into significant relationships will enable them to give and receive care.

Worship is a deep appreciation of God. It is God-centered adoration, praise, thanksgiving and service. Worship is not about what we like. Worship is about what God appreciates. He is the audience; we are the instruments. And He welcomes all forms of expression that flow from a heart overwhelmed with His awesomeness. As leaders we set the climate for worship. Styles of praise, for example, may vary among generational groups. So we encourage both tolerance and commonality to maximize the celebrating of His goodness.

Outreach is presenting Jesus to unbelievers by both word and action. People desperately need to know about God's forgiveness in Christ. And they can best experience this truth by tasting the fruit of love, joy, peace, patience, kindness, goodness, faithfulness, gentleness and self-control in the life of a believing friend (see Galatians 5:22, 23). Effective outreach therefore is person centered, not just soul centered. Outreach is more than evangelism. It is the sharing of our giftedness and resources with those who do not yet know Christ.

People all around us get snagged on the barbwire of life, whether the barbs be broken relationships, unemployment, disease, stress or other challenges. And, sad to say, too many in ministry are wasting their time fussing about media, schedules, facilities and procedures. As leaders we cannot ignore routine concerns. However, we must never let them take center stage. Particular decisions and forms only have meaning as they maximize the Great Commission.

As members of a ministry team, how effective are you in maintaining the priorities of teaching, care giving, worship and outreach? Continue to learn together. Be Christ's healing presence to one another. Celebrate God together in your service. And invite others into the intimacy of Christ. This is His purpose!

Group Exercise:

As a ministry team, your service likely has you engaged more deeply in one of the four purposes than the others (teaching, care-giving, worship and outreach). But on a personal level, which area would you need to pursue more fully in order to nurture overall spiritual growth?

Team Prayer:

Lord, please help us to rise up as the Church of Christ, and truly move beyond lesser things. Frankly, we have spent too much time on the minors. So we commit ourselves now to hold high before Your people our big Kingdom task of teaching, care giving, worship and outreach. Amen!

Final Thought:

Our purpose is to ignite a great commission focus; fueled by a great commandment passion.
— Rick Warren

Leadership Longevity

I myself am convinced, my brothers and sisters, that you yourselves are full of goodness, filled with knowledge and competent to instruct one another. Yet I have written you quite boldly on some points to remind you of them again, because of the grace God gave me to be a minister of Christ Jesus to the Gentiles. He gave me the priestly duty of proclaiming the gospel of God, so that the Gentiles might become an offering acceptable to God, sanctified by the Holy Spirit. Therefore I glory in Christ Jesus in my service to God. I will not venture to speak of anything except what Christ has accomplished through me in leading the Gentiles to obey God by what I have said and done— by the power of signs and wonders, through the power of the Spirit of God. So from Jerusalem all the way around to Illyricum, I have fully proclaimed the gospel of Christ.

— **Romans 15:14–19**

THE MOST DIFFICULT FUNERAL I [John] ever officiated was for a young man who took his own life. He was a Christian, and a number of the people attending the service were teenagers whom he had led to Christ. A Christian's birthright includes joy, peace and hope. But suicide seems a denial of the presence of this fruit in one's life. What went wrong?

This man's younger brother found a diary describing what was going on in his life. Apparently he had been drifting away from the Lord for a while, and had made some decisions that damaged his career and anticipated marriage. In despair, he chose to end his life.

During that week in my devotional reading, I came across 2 Corinthians 11:23-29 where Paul describes his hardships. The apostle worked hard, was imprisoned frequently, flogged severely, brutally whipped five times, beaten with rods three times and even stoned, left for dead. He was in danger from bandits, from his own countrymen and from the Gentiles. He had been shipwrecked, gone without food and sleep, and had been cold and naked. Wow!

I remember asking myself why one person checks out after a few adverse circumstances, while a guy like Paul persisted amidst that amount of hardship. I think some insights can be found from Paul himself. In the Romans passage above, Paul reveals several essentials for leadership longevity.

First, *Paul served with purpose.* He wanted to proclaim the gospel of God to the Gentiles (v. 16), particularly in places where Jesus was not known (v. 20). So for Paul it didn't matter whether he was in the Areopagus, Agrippa's palace, a riverside near Philippi or in prison. He still was able to accomplish his purpose of presenting Christ to unbelievers. No adverse circumstance was large enough to override his personal mission.

Second, *Paul ministered by the power of the Holy Spirit.* Paul's persistence and accomplishments weren't just that of a highly disciplined person. What kept him energized was the Holy Spirit who enabled him to faithfully proclaim the message of Christ. Though he "accomplished" much (v. 18), he was quick to admit that it was "through the power of the Spirit" (v. 19).

Third, *Paul's ministry was bathed in prayer.* Throughout his letters he reminded his recipients that he prayed for them (see, as examples, Romans 1:8-10, Ephesians 1:15–22, or Philippians 1:3-5). Likewise, he invited fellow believers to pray for him. In this same chapter Paul requested his friends' intercession: "Pray that I may be kept safe from the unbelievers in Judea and that the contribution I take to Jerusalem may be favorably received by the Lord's people there" (v. 31).

Fourth, *Paul kept his focus on people.* To these Roman believers he expressed his longing to see them (v. 23). And in his concluding remarks (ch. 16), he sent his personal greetings to many individuals by name. Whether it was Jews or Gentiles, slaves or free or men or women, Paul was concerned with the spiritual nurture of people.

What kept Paul going? It wasn't sheer personal determination. It was his laser focus on his purpose, his sensitivity to and empowerment by the Holy Spirit, his regular communication with the Father through prayer, and his deep connection with teammates.

It is sad that so many people who have previously served Christ are not following Him today. Some have lost their passion, some have become distracted, some have become ensnared and some have become exhausted. As leaders, you'll never face a shortage of needy people and ministry challenges. So plan now to finish well by tapping into Paul's strategy for leadership longevity.

Group Exercise:

In groups of three, answer the following question: Of the four leadership longevity resources (purpose, power, prayer and people), which resource do you need to cultivate most right now. Why?

Pray for the person on your right.

Team Prayer:

Father, it's sobering to look in the pages of Scripture and in the lives of leaders today and see so many who have not finished well. Keep us from putting programs ahead of people. Show us the foolishness of trying to do Your work in our own power. Please give us clarity of purpose, and energize us by Your Spirit. We ask these things in the name of Christ. Amen!

Final Thought:

It doesn't matter if you burn out, rust out, or drop out; you're still out!

Exalting Christ

The Son is the image of the invisible God, the
firstborn over all creation. For in him all things
were created: things in heaven and on earth,
visible and invisible, whether thrones or powers
or rulers or authorities; all things have been
created through him and for him. He is before
all things, and in him all things hold together.
And he is the head of the body, the church; he is
the beginning and the firstborn from among
the dead, so that in everything he might have
the supremacy. For God was pleased to have all
his fullness dwell in him, and through him to
reconcile to himself all things, whether things
on earth or things in heaven, by making peace
through his blood, shed on the cross.

— Colossians 1:15–20

IN CHRISTIAN SERVICE IT'S EASY to get caught up with personal
ministry responsibilities. Whether leading, teaching or caring,
we zero-in on how we can best help others. Nevertheless, while

personal diligence and other-centeredness are commendable, they should not be our primary focus.

The bottom line for all ministry is the exaltation of Christ. We are not teaching a Bible class; we are helping people see the Divine. We are not working with students; we are helping the youth feel the love of God. We are not conducting business; we are praying and deciding how better to make Christ known. We are not running a food shelf; we are helping people sense the compassion of the Bread of Life. And we're not leading a music set; we are exalting God among His people.

This devotional passage of Scripture makes it clear that Jesus Christ is supreme over everything. Creation came into existence through Him, and the universe as we know it is sustained by Him. Both present rulers and unseen powers are under His authority. And by His death on the cross, those who trust Him can be reconciled to God.

Christians are remarkably gifted. This is God's design. All have natural abilities, acquired skills and spiritual gifts. Many, serving with great diligence, have seen fruitful harvests. Yet this, too, is for the glory of God.

Let's never slip into the attitude of Nebuchadnezzar who, while walking on the roof of his royal palace boasted: "Is not this the great Babylon I have built as the royal residence, by my mighty power and for the glory of my majesty?" These words barely came from his mouth when God brought him back down to the earth— literally (see Daniel 4).

When reading this account we may be tempted to think that this kind of self-exaltation, while typical of a pagan, could not happen to a servant of God. But even a humble man like Moses, for example, was not immune to self-exaltation. On one occasion when God asked him to speak to a rock to produce water for the Israelites, he struck the rock and said angrily to the people: "Must we bring you water out of this rock?"

A careful study of the context (Numbers 20:10) reveals that Moses wasn't asking them if he and God should bring water from the rock (a bad enough attitude). He is inquiring if he and Aaron should produce water from the rock (a terrible misrepresentation). In reality, only Jehovah was Israel's Provider. Moses' impetuous act prevented Aaron and him from entering the Promised Land.

A God-exalting attitude recognizes that the salvation we enjoy is at His initiative: "For it is by grace you have been saved, through faith and this not from yourselves, it is the gift of God not of works, so that no one can boast" (Ephesians 2:8, 9). A God-exalting attitude further recognizes that whether we have "two, five or ten talents," all that we enjoy is from God's gracious hand.

Therefore, as leaders, always use your giftedness with great diligence for Christ's pleasure. May your service to others never be the end focus. Through your teamwork may you know the joy of helping others exalt Christ.

Group Exercise:

Identify better ways to do a better job of exalting Christ among those we serve?

Team Prayer:

Father, keep us from a false kind of humility
that refuses to acknowledge the rich giftedness
with which You have blessed each of us. At the
same time, we ask that You would allow us to
always use that giftedness to lift up Christ. Help
us to attend diligently to our teamwork, but
always with the long view in mind— that of
exalting Your Son. Amen!

Final Thought:

If people do not exalt Christ,
the stones will cry out in adoration.

— Luke 19:40

Priorities

Now the Passover and the Festival of Unleavened
Bread were only two days away, and the chief
priests and the teachers of the law were looking
for some sly way to arrest Jesus and kill him.
'But not during the Festival,' they said, 'or the
people may riot.' While he was in Bethany,
reclining at the table in the home of Simon the
Leper, a woman came with an alabaster jar of
very expensive perfume, made of pure nard. She
broke the jar and poured the perfume on his head.
Some of those present were saying indignantly
to one another, 'Why this waste of perfume?
It could have been sold for more than a year's
wages and the money given to the poor.' And
they rebuked her harshly. 'Leave her alone,' said
Jesus. 'Why are you bothering her? She has done
a beautiful thing to me. The poor you will always
have with you, and you can help them any time

you want. But you will not always have me.
She did what she could. She poured perfume on
my body beforehand to prepare for my burial.
Truly I tell you, wherever the gospel is preached
throughout the world, what she has done will also
be told, in memory of her.' Then Judas Iscariot,
one of the Twelve, went to the chief priests to
betray Jesus to them.

— Mark 14:1–10

WHEN JESUS TRAVELED NEAR JERUSALEM He often stayed in the home of His friends Mary, Martha and Lazarus. On one occasion Martha was preparing the meal while Mary was sitting and listening to Jesus. In Luke 10:38-42 we are told that Martha was upset because Mary left her to do all the work. Martha wanted Jesus to reprimand Mary.

Jesus' response to Martha did not minimize the need for people to prepare meals— that's a necessary part of life. But He did use the occasion to teach Martha, and us, the importance of priorities: "Mary has chosen what is better, and it will not be taken away from her." At any given moment, some things are just more important than other things.

Mary's appreciation, love and reverence for Jesus were displayed on another occasion. In the devotional passage above we observe Jesus in the town of Bethany visiting in the home of a man named Simon. Mary interrupted the gathering by pouring a jar of expensive perfume on the head of Jesus (Mark 14:3). Some of those present expressed their indignation at this wasteful act. Judas questioned: "Why wasn't this perfume sold and the money given to the poor? It was worth a year's wages" (John 14:5). In reply, Jesus made it clear that there are always opportunities to help the poor, but only this moment to anoint Him: "You will not always have me. She poured perfume on my body beforehand to prepare for my burial" (Mark 14:7, 8).

An important word often overlooked in Jesus' response is the word *beforehand*. Someone has stated that too many of us are *behindhand* Christians. We neglect to prioritize our actions and decisions. Only later do we realize that we missed a great opportunity. Living by priorities is important in all of life. Responsible living requires that each day we make choices on how we invest out time, abilities and finances.

But by way of immediate application, consider how prioritization can even influence your present meeting. Too often at team sessions an inordinate amount of time is spent dealing with pressing, yet less important matters. Then, unfortunately, because the clock keeps moving, important concerns get tabled until future meetings. Too often, the urgent crowds out the important.

Prioritizing gives precedence to time, order and significance. Not everything is equally important. In our ministry service, and even at our team meetings, it is necessary to prioritize the things that we *must do*, what we *should do*, and finally what we *hope to do*.

Group Exercise:

Look at your meeting agenda, or create an agenda if you do not have one.

Check the items, and reorder them if necessary, to give priority to the most important things.

Team Prayer:

Lord, we often get frustrated because we don't
seem to have the time needed to do everything
we want to do. Help us understand that we all
have the same amount of time. Give us wisdom
and discernment to tackle the important items
we face. And above all, help us to remember that
our greatest priority is always keeping You first.
Amen!

Final Thought:

God, give us grace to accept with Serenity the
things that cannot be changed, Courage to
change the things which should be changed, and
the Wisdom to distinguish the one from the other.
— **Reinhold Niebuhr**

Commitment

Do not fret because of those who are evil or be
envious of those who do wrong; for like the grass
they will soon wither, like green plants they will
soon die away. Trust in the LORD and do good;
dwell in the land and enjoy safe pasture. Take
delight in the LORD and he will give you the
desires of your heart. Commit your way to the
LORD; trust in him and he will do this: he will
make your righteous reward shine like the dawn,
your vindication like the noonday sun. Be still
before the LORD and wait patiently for him; do
not fret when people succeed in their ways, when
they carry out their wicked schemes.

— Psalm 37:1–7

A TEENAGER ASKED IF I [Fred] would play racquetball with him.
We arranged a time for me to pick him up and bring him back
home. We had a good time, and I felt as if we were able to relate
to one another. The next Sunday his mother, a single parent,
thanked me. Surprisingly, she didn't thank me for taking time

to play with her son, instead she said, "You are the first man who promised my son something and then kept his commitment."

What a commentary on the lack of commitment in our society. I wondered what kind of father and husband this teenager would be if he eventually married and had a family. Commitment was not modeled for him.

Over the past few decades people seem to be less willing to make long-term commitments. This is observable in that:

- ◆ Fewer people are willing to join book and CD clubs
- ◆ Volunteers are less willing to accept annual appointments to ministry
- ◆ Consumers are less loyal to specific brands
- ◆ Membership in organizations, including churches, is declining

Some people struggle with any kind of commitment, and an increasing number avoid long-term commitments altogether.

Another area of life in which a lack of commitment is obvious is marriage. Cohabitation has escalated, leading to the deferral of marriage, and in some cases the elimination of marriage. The divorce rate has also climbed; people are more willing to bail out than to work it out. Some couples, desiring to alter the traditional vows, have inserted, as long "as we both shall love." Apparently, vows are not terminated by death, but by a current state of mind. Many people prefer vows of conscience to vows of commitment.

A non-committal attitude is reflected in people's relationships to ministry as well. The emphasis has switched from permanent and long-term, to temporary and short-term. People change churches, for example, almost as often as the places they choose to shop.

In the devotional passage above, God instructs His people on how to live Godly lives. First, they should not be distracted by those who do wrong, but instead be focused on the Lord. By trusting in Him, people find joy and safety (v. 3). By delighting in Him, the desires of their heart come to fulfillment (v. 4). By committing their way to the Lord, they shine with purpose (v. 6). By waiting patiently for Him, they prosper and enjoy great peace (vv. 7, 11). This psalm is a reminder of the importance of commitment.

John Bode penned the words to the beautiful hymn, O *Jesus I Have Promised*. The first verse declares: "O Jesus I have promised to serve You to the end; be now and ever near me my Master and my friend. I shall not fear the battle if You are by my side, nor wander from the pathway if You will be my guide." I have sung that hymn many times. Isn't one time enough to say, I promise? Not really. Our commitment needs to be renewed throughout the span of our lives and ministry.

Perhaps today is a good time to renew your commitment to serve God to the end. If we want to be successful in our ministry, we need to make a total commitment. This includes not only the length of time, but also the intentional involvement of our heart and mind.

Group Exercise:

Identify some barriers to commitment,
particularly in Kingdom service.

What might help people 'commit their way' to the
Lord more deeply?

Team Prayer:

Our faithful, heavenly Father, thank You for
Your steadfast commitment to us as leaders. We
are grateful for the confidence that You have
placed in us as Your children, as Your servants
and as Your friends. We renew our promise to be
wholly committed to You throughout our Years of
service. Amen!

Final Thought:

Old Faithful is not the largest geyser, nor does
it reach the greatest height. Nevertheless, it is by
far the most popular geyser. Its popularity is due
mainly to its regularity and dependability.

— **Wallace Fridy**

Vision

Do not store up for yourselves treasures on earth,
where moth and rust destroy, and where thieves
break in and steal. But store up for yourselves
treasures in heaven, where moth and rust do not
destroy, and where thieves do not break in and
steal. For where your treasure is, there your heart
will be also. The eye is the lamp of the body. If
your eyes are healthy, your whole body will be
full of light. But if your eyes are unhealthy,
your whole body will be full of darkness. If then
the light within you is darkness, how great is
that darkness! No one can serve two masters.
Either you will hate the one and love the other,
or you will be devoted to the one and despise the
other. You cannot serve both God and Money.

— Matthew 6:19–24

A FRIEND OF MINE [JOHN], an ophthalmologist, was asked to
read the eye chart without his glasses. He guessed at a few
letters then inquired, "How did I do?" The doctor responded,

"They are numbers!" Needless to say, without his glasses, he couldn't see much.

Likewise, as Christ followers, without looking through the lenses of Jesus, we don't see clearly; we are nearsighted to what God is doing around us. We too naturally notice, and get consumed, by the stuff of the material world. But when we do so, we miss more important matters in life.

Observe some classical cases of spiritual myopia recorded in the Scriptures:

- When Eve *saw* the fruit of the tree, she desired it. She thought it was good for food and would give her wisdom. But her disobedience to God resulted in the Fall (Genesis 3:6).

- When the sons of God *saw* the daughters of earth, they desired them. Part of the result of this illicit relationship was the flood (Gen 6:2).

- When the Israeli spies *saw* the giants of Anak, they were afraid and presented a bad report to the Israelites. Their myopia resulted in the Israelites wandering in the wilderness for 40 years (Numbers 13:28).

- When Achan *saw* the spoils in Jericho, he coveted some items and hid them in his tent. His stealing of the *devoted* items resulted in Israel's defeat by the men of Ai (Joshua 7:21).

- When Samson *saw* a young Philistine woman, he told his dad he had to have her. We all know the personal pain he experienced because of Delilah (Judges 14:1).

- When David *saw* a woman bathing, he desired her and took her. This midlife leader, with too much time on his hands, became guilty of adultery and murder because of his covetous vision (2 Samuel 11:2).

What a contrast is seen through the eyes of Jesus. Christ consistently noticed people, particularly the needy:

◆ When Jesus *saw* a woman in a funeral procession, His heart went out to her. Filled with compassion, He restored her son's life. And all the people were "filled with awe and praised God" (Luke 7:13).

◆ When Jesus *looked up* and saw Zacchaeus, He told him that He would like to visit with him in his home. The result was that Zacchaeus became a follower, and generously distributed much of his wealth (Luke 19:5).

◆ When Jesus *saw* a cripple woman in a synagogue, He called her forward and healed her. "Immediately she straightened up and praised God" (Luke 13:12).

◆ When Jesus *saw* a crowd that was hungry, He had compassion on them and fed them. The result was that more than 5,000 received bread from the Bread of Life, the miracle authenticating the messenger (Matthew 14:14).

◆ In Jesus' parable, when a father *saw* a prodigal son, he was filled with compassion for him. The result was restoration of a wayward son (Luke 15:20).

In the first cluster of examples, the people's nearsightedness produced devastating results. By way of contrast, Jesus' unselfish vision let Him see into the hearts of people, transforming their lives.

As leaders, let's consciously make an effort to see through the lenses of Jesus. Perhaps during the week you can consider further these additional passages that tell us what we should *look at* or *see*. Our vision will be sharpened when we:

- ◆ See our own shortcomings (Matthew 7:3–5)
- ◆ See God's great mercy (Matthew 18:32)
- ◆ Observe God's watch care (Matthew 6:26)
- ◆ See the disadvantaged (Matthew 25:37–40)
- ◆ See the spiritually injured (1 John 5:16)
- ◆ See the interest of others (Philippians 2:4)
- ◆ See opportunities for ministry (John 4:35)
- ◆ See the Day drawing near (Hebrews 10:25; 2 Timothy 3:1–5)

Group Exercise:

Share a time when you saw a ministry opportunity and embraced it, or a time when in hindsight you recognized you missed a service opportunity.

Team Prayer:

Father, give us the vision of Your dear Son, Jesus. Keep us from spiritual injuries due to shortsightedness. Help us to view possessions as less significant, and see people as more important. May the lenses we look through reveal the view of Christ. Amen!

Final Thought:

Let us fix our eyes on Jesus, the pioneer and perfecter of faith, who, for the joy set before Him endured the cross, scorning its shame, and sat down at the right hand of the throne of God. Consider Him who endured such opposition from sinners, so that you will not grow weary and lose heart.

— **Hebrews 12:2, 3**

God's Constancy

God is not a human, that he should lie,
not a human being, that he should change his
mind. Does he speak and then not act? Does he
promise and not fulfill?
— Numbers 23:19

CHRISTIANS IN THE 21ST CENTURY are living in a sea surge of change. For example, in the 90's fuel was relatively inexpensive, world economies seemed stable, terrorism wasn't a global concern and the internet was in its infancy. Today, our *global village* is rocked by meteorological threats, unpredictable economic cycles, international terrorism and biotechnical breakthroughs.

In the world of congregational life, we also have experienced change. Dotting the landscape are traditional churches, seeker churches, emergent churches, mega-churches, meta-churches, postmodern churches, house churches and multi-site churches. In addition, a growing wave of parachurch organizations, market place ministries and not-for-profit corporations are offering a swell in Christian products and services.

With so much changing around us, it is easy to become unsettled in life and uncertain in ministry direction. Therefore, from time to time it is important to refresh our perspective and refocus on that which transcends the situational and temporal. A reminder of God's constancy helps us reconnect to the timeless and regain perspective.

First, let's remember that *God is unchanging in His personhood*. Songs like *Amazing Grace* and *How Great Thou Art* remind us of the constancy of God's nature. His love wasn't just great yesterday; it is great right now, and will also be great in the future (Psalm 100:5). His mercy wasn't just a passing quality; it is His ongoing character (Luke 1:50). His presence is everywhere (Hebrews 13:5); His power is unlimited (Job 42:2); and His knowledge is absolute (Matthew 6:8). Because God is unalterable, His character qualities remain constant.

Second, let's affirm that *God is unchanging in His plans*. What God says He will do, He will do. "The Lord Almighty has sworn, 'Surely, as I have planned, so it will be, and as I have purposed, so it will happen'" (Isaiah 14:24). God did not create the world, and then turn it loose. He did not create you, and then leave you alone. And He did not bring the Church together just to let it run by itself. God remains deeply engaged with His creation. Believers can have assurance of faith because God, in His constancy, cannot change the plan of salvation.

Third, let's rejoice that *God is unchanging in His provision*. He always has the well-being of His children in mind. In James we read: "Every good and perfect gift is from above, coming down from the Father of heavenly lights, who does not change like shifting shadows" (James 1:17). Because of His immutable wisdom, knowledge and power, God delivers on His promises. His provision includes forgiveness (1 John 1:9), wisdom (James 1:5), comfort (2 Corinthians 1:3-5) and peace (Philippians 4:7). And we have the assurance that, "in all things God works for the good of those who love Him, who have been called according to His purpose" (Romans 8:28).

As you work together as a ministry team, be reminded that God is unchanging, that His Word is reliable and that His mission is uncompromising. At the same time, also enjoy the privilege that He gives you to present this unchanging message in creative ways to an ever-changing culture. Finally, take joy in His unending love and faithfulness as you serve together as a team.

Group Exercise:

What character quality of God do you most appreciate at this present time? Why?

Team Prayer:

FATHER, thank You for Your unchanging nature. You are the same yesterday, today and forever. Your character remains constant, therefore Your love, mercy and trustworthiness are always there for us. Your purposes remain the same; therefore You continue to reconcile people to Yourself. And Your promises remain the same; therefore we can count on You to fulfill Your good intentions. Please forgive us for our fallibility.

Help us to be more like You— consistent and trustworthy. Amen!

Final Thought:

Oh God, our help in ages past, our hope for years to come, Be Thou our guide while life shall last, and our eternal home.

— Isaac Watts

This meditation has been adapted from John R. Cionca's article, "God Is Immutable—The Constancy of His Nature," in *Decision Magazine*, January, 1990: © 1989 Billy Graham Evangelistic Association; used by permission, all rights reserved.

Sabbath

One Sabbath Jesus was going through the grainfields, and as his disciples walked along, they began to pick some heads of grain. The Pharisees said to him, 'Look, why are they doing what is unlawful on the Sabbath?' He answered, 'have you never read what David did when he and his companions were hungry and in need? In the days of Abiathar the high priest, he entered the house of God and ate the consecrated bread, which is lawful only for priests to eat. And he also gave some to his companions.' Then he said to them, 'The Sabbath was made for people, not people for the Sabbath. So the Son of Man is Lord even of the Sabbath.'

— Mark 2:23–28

DOES ANYONE ON YOUR MINISTRY team feel like they have too much time on their hands? Anyone wishing that they could be busier? I doubt it! Most people work nearly 50 hours per week on the job. In addition they have family, church and community activities. Everything from cleaning the house to renewing your vehicle registration competes for your meager discretionary time.

As believers we would not intentionally dishonor the Lord. We want our lifestyle to reflect the Sermon on the Mount; we want to keep the Ten Commandments. Interestingly, the fourth commandment (Exodus 20:8–11) requires God's people to rest, yet in our task-oriented, productivity-esteeming culture, even Christians too often run their lives with little margin.

In this devotional passage we observe Jesus' critics accusing him of law breaking because the disciples were picking and eating grain along their journey. In order to protect the Sabbath, the Jewish teachers developed an extensive list of regulations and restrictions. According to the specifics in their *Mishnah*, the Pharisees accused the disciples of *sifting, threshing, winnowing* and even *eating with unclean hands.*

Note that Jesus did not minimize or suggest an elimination of the Sabbath principle. He would be familiar with the Old Testament law. He understood that there was a two-fold purpose of the Sabbath (see Leviticus 23:1–3). First, it was a day to refrain from routine labor. This special day was not a time for catch-up. Second, it was a day set aside for sacred assembly. The faith community could gather together each week to celebrate God's goodness.

The Creator has not wired His creation to go 24/7. Discouragement and unrest because of fatigue and time pressure is rampant. And while fruitfulness and productivity are esteemed in Scripture, workaholism is an insult to the Creator, who Himself rested on the seventh day.

When confronted by the Pharisees, Jesus corrected their misunderstanding of the principle. He affirmed that "the Sabbath was made for people, not people for the Sabbath" (v. 27). In other words, God's command was not to weigh us down with a list of rules and regulations. It was to free us up from wearing ourselves down by unceasing work. It is there to provide rest and relaxation. The Sabbath texts remind us of the need for celebration and recharging. This special day, which is given weekly, is a gift of release from work and a blessing of regular renewal.

As leaders and as friends, make a commitment today to hold each other accountable to gain more margin in your lives. Put the principle of Sabbath into practice, and see if you do not experience renewal and refreshment and a richer sense of the Father's presence. This one-day-out-of-seven change of pace may be on a Saturday (literal Sabbath) or on Sunday, or even during another day of the week. But by limiting our to-do list to six days, we receive the Creator's blessing of rest.

Group Exercise:

Share with one another an activity you enjoy that helps you recharge.

When can you next schedule it?

Team Prayer:

Father, thank You for providing for us in so many ways. We know that work is good, for it is part of what You established in the garden even before the Fall. However, we confess that we have allowed job responsibilities, and at times the pursuit of wealth, to take preeminence in our lives. We have let the urgent crowd out the important. We have let the temporal overshadow the eternal. And we have let the personal accomplishing of tasks squeeze out relational time with You and others. Today we commit ourselves to regaining margin. Let us not be like the Pharisees who were legalistic and inflexible. But also give us the discipline to restrict our work and chores to six days. Help us to guard against the barrenness of a busy life. Amen!

Final Thought:

Come to Me, all you who are weary and burdened, and I will give you rest.

— Jesus, in Matthew 11:28

Credit

Therefore if you have any encouragement from being united with Christ, if any comfort from his love, if any common sharing in the Spirit, if any tenderness and compassion, then make my joy complete by being like-minded, having the same love, being one in spirit and of one mind. Do nothing out of selfish ambition or vain conceit. Rather, in humility value others above yourselves, not looking to your own interests but each of you to the interests of the others. In your relationships with one another, have the same attitude of mind Christ Jesus had: Who, being in very nature God, did not consider equality with God something to be used to his own advantage; rather, he made himself nothing by taking the very nature of a servant, being made in human likeness. And being found in appearance as a human being, he humbled himself by becoming obedient to death— even death on a cross! Therefore God exalted him to the highest place

> and gave him the name that is above every name,
> that at the name of Jesus every knee should bow,
> in heaven and on earth and under the earth, and
> every tongue acknowledge that Jesus Christ is
> Lord, to the glory of God the Father.
> — Philippians 2:1–11

WHILE SERVING ON A PARACHURCH staff, I [Fred] designed a program plan for a series of meetings. However, my boss presented my plan as if the design and material were his own ideas, never acknowledging, publicly or privately, that the work behind the presentation was mine. I must admit, his lack of recognition resulted in my lack of joy.

Yet what a contrast of attitude we find in the above scripture passage. In it we see a wonderful example of the joy received when no recognition is given.

To the Philippians, and to us, Paul describes the self-emptying attitude of our Savior. Jesus did not give up His deity, but willingly laid aside His eternal glory so that He could identify with humanity. He became a servant by humbling Himself. He died a criminal's death even though He was an innocent man. He temporarily gave up His power and position in order to point people to His Heavenly Father. Although He is God, Jesus joyfully came to earth, "not to be served, but to serve" (Mark 10:45).

In verses one through four of this passage, Paul challenges believers to become like-minded. He exhorts the church to have the same attitude as Jesus Christ to lay aside ourselves in order to lift up the Lord.

Someone has suggested that joy in the Christian life becomes a reality when you consider yourself third:

Jesus – first

Others – second

Yourself – third

The Apostle Paul urges: "Do nothing out of selfish ambition or vain conceit, but in humility consider others better than yourselves" (v. 3). Offering recognition for the contributions of others is a great practice. Hearing a word of affirmation is always appreciated. But looking for recognition for our own contributions is a detrimental expectation. Our greatest joy will be realized on that day when God Himself offers the commendation, "Well done, good and faithful servant" (Matthew 25:21).

As members of a leadership team, don't worry about who gets the credit for an event or activity. Instead, "serve wholeheartedly, as if you were serving the Lord" (Ephesians 6:7). After all, it is God who has graced and gifted each member of the team (James 1:17). As the hymn writer so beautifully declared, "To God be the Glory, Great Things He Hath Done!"

Group Exercise:

Upon whose shoulders are you standing? Identify someone who has positively influenced your life.

Team Prayer:

You, Lord, are worthy to receive all honor and glory. Thank you for bringing us together for this ministry. The sum of all our gifts and abilities is multiplied as we submit them to Your control. Help us to serve faithfully as we submit to You and to one another through the presence and power of the Holy Spirit in our lives. Amen!

Final Thought:

You can have any idea you want, as long as you don't care who gets the credit and God gets the glory.

Criticism

Woe to you when everyone speaks well of you,
for that is how their ancestors treated the false
prophets. 'But to you who are listening I say:
Love your enemies, do good to those who hate
you, bless those who curse you, pray for those
who mistreat you. If someone slaps you on one
cheek, turn the other also. If someone takes your
coat, do not withhold your shirt. Give to everyone
who asks you, and if anyone takes what belongs
to you, do not demand it back. Do to others as
you would have them do to you. 'If you love those
who love you, what credit is that to you? Even
sinners love those who love them. And if you do
good to those who are good to you, what credit is
that to you? Even sinners do that. And if you
lend to those from whom you expect repayment,
what credit is that to you? Even sinners lend
to sinners, expecting to be repaid in full. But
love your enemies, do good to them, and lend to
them without expecting to get anything back.

> Then your reward will be great, and you will be
> children of the Most High, because he is kind to
> the ungrateful and wicked. Be merciful, just as
> your Father is merciful.
>
> — Luke 6:26–36

A GRANDFATHER AND HIS GRANDSON began a journey to the next village early in the day. They packed a few possessions and a lunch and placed them on their donkey.

As they walked through a neighboring village, they overheard two women talking: "Why isn't someone riding that donkey? Those two will be exhausted before they get where they are going."

So when they reached the edge of the village, the grandfather told the boy to ride on the donkey. Before they had gone much farther they heard two passers-by saying: "Why is that boy riding the donkey? He should let the old man ride. The old man looks so tired."

The two exchanged places. Yet when they reached the next town someone shouted to the old man: "Why are you riding the donkey and making the boy walk? Both of you should be riding the donkey." So the grandfather sat the boy next to him on the donkey to continue the journey.

As they entered the next village someone hollered: "Why are you both riding that donkey? Poor donkey. You'll wear him out." So they got off the donkey and walked alongside the animal.

When they finally reached their destination, they felt weary from the journey and frustrated from all the criticism. However, they learned a valuable lesson.

As a young pastor I [Fred] tried my best to avoid criticism. I would spend most of my Mondays apologizing for things for which I had been criticized on the previous day. But the harder I worked, the more frustrated I got. It seemed that no matter what I did, someone always second guessed or criticized my direction or performance. Then one day I read Luke 6:26, "Woe to you when everyone speaks well of you," and I began to realize that trying to please everyone could actually become a liability.

Some people react negatively to criticism by defensively fighting back. Others let the criticism drain their drive and self-confidence. However, there is a third option. Executive coaches tell leaders that whenever they are criticized, they should ask themselves, "Is there a kernel of truth in this criticism?" If so, we can learn from the element of truth that is present, and then move beyond it to lead with new insight. Criticism, in essence, can foster growth.

No one likes to be criticized. Yet all leaders in ministry will eventually discover that criticism comes with the position. When criticism comes your way, pray that it won't make you bitter, but rather better. Don't be surprised by criticism, and don't allow it to thwart your Spirit-led leadership.

Group Exercise:

Share an example of a criticism that became a tool for growth in your life.

What helped you move beyond the criticism?

Team Prayer:

Dear Father, we confess that we desire to be loved and accepted by everyone whom we seek to serve. It is good to be reminded that even Your beloved Son was criticized by His own people. Help us constantly to remember that our aim is to please You. Amen!

Final Thought:

Neither let criticism surprise you, nor let it control you.

Delegation

The next day Moses took his seat to serve as judge for the people, and they stood around him from morning till evening. When his father-in-law saw all that Moses was doing for the people, he said, 'What is this you are doing for the people? Why do you alone sit as judge, while all these people stand around you from morning till evening?' Moses answered him, 'Because the people come to me to seek God's will. Whenever they have a dispute, it is brought to me, and I decide between the parties and inform them of God's decrees and instructions.' Moses' father-in-law replied, 'What you are doing is not good. You and these people who come to you will only wear yourselves out. The work is too heavy for you; you cannot handle it alone. Listen now to me and I will give you some advice, and may God be with you. You must be the people's representative before God and bring their disputes to him. Teach them his decrees and instructions, and show

them the way they are to live and how they are
to behave. But select capable men from all the
people— men who fear God, trustworthy men
who hate dishonest gain— and appoint them as
officials over thousands, hundreds, fifties and
tens. Have them serve as judges for the people at
all times, but have them bring every difficult
case to you; the simple cases they can decide
themselves. That will make your load lighter,
because they will share it with you. If you do
this and God so commands, you will be able to
stand the strain, and all these people will go home
satisfied.'

— Exodus 18:13–23

WHETHER YOU ARE SERVING IN a paid ministry position
or in a volunteer capacity, you probably have more things to
accomplish each day than you have day in which to complete
them. This situation is typical for most people because:

- ◆ Global awareness has expanded our world
- ◆ 21st century lifestyles are busy
- ◆ Technology, while helpful, requires continual learning
- ◆ People have real and complex needs
- ◆ Transformation happens best only through quality of
  time investments

While all the above conditions are a present reality, having
more work than day is not novel to the 21st century. In the
scripture text above, for example, we see that Moses faced the
same leadership challenge some 3,500 years ago. The context of
this narrative is subsequent to the Exodus, when the Israelites

were traveling through the Sinai wilderness. Moses was God's appointed leader for their journey to the Promised Land.

When his father-in-law came to visit him, he noticed that Moses was serving as the sole arbiter for the whole community. Jethro quickly recognized the futility of this approach, and told Moses that he could not stand as judge alone (v. 14). No doubt he saw the toll this practice was taking on his son-in-law (v. 18). So he advised Moses to select capable leaders who could assist him (v. 21a). He further explained a plan for the division of labor which shared the responsibility across manageable work teams (v. 21b).

The anticipated result of this distributive work would be relief for Moses (v. 23a), and resolve for the people (v. 23b). Effective delegation had a positive effect on Moses (refreshment), on the leaders (use of their gifts) and on the people (satisfaction of their concerns). The bottom line is that the synergy of teamwork is more powerful than the solo accomplishments of even a star performer. Simply stated, effective delegation leads to more effective outcomes.

Delegation is not the dumping of work by one person onto another. I [John] recall a situation where one leader came into a subordinate's office and piled a stack of folders in front of him. On the way out the door, the boss snickered: "Ha-ha, that's my job—getting work off my desk and onto yours." The recipient felt demeaned; not like a colleague. This poor understanding of delegation eroded team loyalty.

So when should we delegate? First, we should invite others to co-labor with us *in areas of our non-strengths*. Each of us has a gift mix. Some people, for example, are creative, innovate, big picture thinkers; others are consistent, conscientious, detailed planners. Inviting others to share in responsibilities outside of our strengths leads to greater ministry effectiveness.

A second way to delegate is to release to others *the things that they can do well*, irrespective of our giftedness. Even in areas of personal competence, if others have a strong gift mix in these areas, include them in the division of labor. This practice always produces better results.

One could argue that effective delegation means giving everything away. The breadth of people's needs and the depth of work required for spiritual transformation require teams of people serving passionately out of their giftedness. And Ephesians 4:11–13 reminds leaders that their primary task is to "equip people for works of service."

Therefore, the mark of your effectiveness as a leader will not primarily be the number of people you personally touched, but the multiple lives touched through the additional leaders that your team develops.

Group Exercise:

What is one thing for which you are responsible that, frankly, is out of your giftedness sweet spot? Offer suggestions to one another of people who can potentially assist with this work.

Team Prayer:

Father, it's easy to admit that there are more needs out there than we have time to address. Yet while we focus on the needs of those under our care, help us to also see and invite into the journey others who You are calling into service. Let us not push on them the responsibilities that we should own, but help us to share with others the work that they can do more effectively. May You be pleased through our collaborative service. Amen!

Final Thought:

It is better to get 10 men to work than to do the work of 10 men!

— **D L Moody**

Only You!

For it is by grace you have been saved, through faith— and this is not from yourselves, it is the gift of God— not by works, so that no one can boast. For we are God's handiwork, created in Christ Jesus to do good works, which God prepared in advance for us to do.

— Ephesians 2:8–10

PERHAPS THE BEST LEADERSHIP ADVICE I've [John] ever heard is: First, always remain a student of the scriptures, and second, always be a student of the culture. But let me add one more area of focus— always be a student of yourself! In other words, each of you will make the most impact in ministry when you operate out of the unique composite of what God has woven into your lives. Let me pass on three thoughts along this line.

First, *recognize your uniqueness*. Look at any group of people and you will realize that each person is physically unique. Even identical twins have their subtle differences. No one else has your fingerprints; no one else has your DNA. That should tell you something.

You are also psychologically unique. Millions of people may be extroverts, or creative, or reflective. Nevertheless, if you were to take the *StrengthsFinder, 16* PF, MMPI, or the *Meyers-Briggs*, no one would match your personality across those instruments. Again, that should tell you something.

And experientially you are unique. The family that you entered was a different family than the one your brother or sister entered. While many people have had similar experiences, you have had a series of experiences that have imprinted the way you make decisions, interact with others and choose to live your life. Some of those experiences were great; some difficult; and some painful. And the Bible assures us that, no matter what the experience, God uses it in our lives (Romans 8:28). Again, that should tell you something.

If nobody else looks like you, no one else is psychologically wired like you, and no one else has had the same life experiences as you, I think it's safe to give up the cloning game and just be yourself.

So first, *take some time for personal reflection and assessment.* Utilize personality inventories and leadership style instruments for better insight into yourself and how you come across to others. Take advantage of the good resources out there to help you get a more complete picture of yourself.

Second, *respond to your giftedness.* God has blessed you with many gifts and abilities. Some of your colleagues are musical, others are great with their hands, some are coordinated and others are funny. You have been given many natural abilities, you have acquired skills, and God has endowed you with spiritual gifts. It matters little how or when a particular ability was added to your gift mix. The bottom line is that whatever we do, we're to do it all for the glory of God (1 Corinthians 10:31). So look for ways to maximize not only the personality and background that God has provided you, but also the many talents that He has woven into your life.

Third, *refuse comparison.* A woman approached me after one of our services and said: "John, you know that I'm in this church because of your preaching, but you're not my favorite preacher— Charles Stanley is." I responded: "Eleanor, that's okay. If God wanted me to be Charles Stanley, he would have had me born to Mama Stanley. Instead, he had me born to Mama Cionca. And that's just fine."

When I hear the poor preaching of some pastors, I wish their congregations could have me instead. However, when I hear the preaching of great communicators, I think, "my poor people," and I want to return my ordination certificate! The comparison game can kill us.

Do you remember when Peter asked Jesus: "What about him, Lord?" (John 21:21) Jesus responded: "What's that to you, you follow Me." What matters is not how many talents you have— ten? five? two?— but how faithful you are in utilizing what God has given to you. God is responsible for how He has gifted other team members. So let's focus on how He's wired us.

What an incredible privilege is ours— serving Christ by serving His people. So just let the sovereign God who designed each of you and brought you this far continue to work through your individual uniqueness. For in God's planning, like with

Queen Esther, no doubt, you have come to your position "for such a time as this" (Esther 4:14b).

Group Exercise:

What has been one experience you have had that no one else (or few) have had?

Team Prayer:

Dear Lord, help us to recognize the blessing of uniqueness that You have given to each one on this ministry team. Thanks for our differences. And thanks that more people can be touched by our team because of our complementary wiring. May You receive much honor as we serve You through the personalities, giftedness and experiences that You have woven into our lives. Amen!

Final Thought:

God made me fast, and when I run I feel His pleasure.
— Eric Liddle, in Chariots of Fire

Reprinted from *Dear Pastor: Ministry Advice from Seasoned Pastors* with permission of Group Publishing, Inc.

Disagreement

Some time later Paul said to Barnabas, 'Let us go back and visit the believers in all the towns where we preached the word of the Lord and see how they are doing.' Barnabas wanted to take John, also called Mark, with them, but Paul did not think it wise to take him, because he had deserted them in Pamphylia and had not continued with them in the work. They had such a sharp disagreement that they parted company. Barnabas took Mark and sailed for Cyprus, but Paul chose Silas and left, commended by the believers to the grace of the Lord. He went through Syria and Cilicia, strengthening the churches.

— Acts 15:36–41

WOULDN'T IT BE GREAT TO be part of a team of leaders in a church or parachurch organization who agreed on everything? While that may sound good, in reality it's not only unrealistic, but could prove detrimental to a team.

Ruth Graham, late wife of world-renowned evangelist, Billy Graham, was once asked if she agreed with her husband on everything. "No, I don't," she replied. "If two people agree on everything, one of them isn't necessary."

Even the leaders in the early church had their disagreements. For example, in Acts 15 we read that Paul and Barnabas had such a sharp disagreement they parted company. Even though they had previously worked well together, they came to an impasse over the composition of their team for the second missionary journey.

The cause of their disagreement was whether or not to include John Mark on their team. Task-oriented Paul believed strongly that their mission would be compromised by including Mark. On their first missionary journey Mark left them to go back home. Relationally-oriented Barnabas, on the other hand, thought the young man deserved another chance. As a result both men built new teams and went on separate mission outreaches.

It would be easy to speculate as to who was right or wrong in this disagreement. However, it is interesting to read in 2 Timothy 4:1 that Paul, in his later years, wanted Mark on his team: "Get Mark and bring him with you, because he is helpful to me in my ministry." Apparently, the additional years of mentorship under Barnabas strengthened the emerging leader.

Periodic disagreements are a reality and a challenge to teams. Therefore, remembering our many agreements keeps our differences in perspective. In this spirit Paul advised the church at Philippi: "Make me truly happy by agreeing with each other, loving one another, and working together with one heart and purpose" (2:2, NLT). When disagreements are resolved, restoration and new ministry possibilities can happen.

Paul urges leaders to agree with one another. As team members you need to agree on the mission and objectives you are working to achieve. You must also agree on your purpose to glorify God through your attitudes, actions and aspirations.

As you move toward the goal of glorifying God through your focused ministry, the by-product of fellowship will draw you closer to each other. And as you come to know one another better, you will grow in appreciation for the unique contribution that each member brings to the team.

Agreement in the essential areas of ministry does not come automatically or easily. All leaders must spend time in prayer, examining their hearts to make certain their desire is to be Christ-like in all deliberations and decisions. When this happens, your work together as a team will be more rewarding.

Group Exercise:

In a circle response, identify on a scale of 1 – 5 (5 being very comfortable) how comfortable you are with disagreement in a team setting. Respect one another's honest responses. What could help your team disagree more agreeably?

Team Prayer:

Dear Lord, help us to recognize and respect the differences represented by individuals in this room. We realize it is humanly impossible to agree on everything. May we not seek our own rights and interests but humbly and lovingly seek to fulfill the task You have given us. Amen!

Final Thought:

Begin each meeting by agreeing to disagree agreeably.

An Open Door to a New World

But mark this: There will be terrible times in
the last days. People will be lovers of themselves,
lovers of money, boastful, proud, abusive,
disobedient to their parents, ungrateful, unholy,
without love, unforgiving, slanderous, without
self-control, brutal, not lovers of the good,
treacherous, rash, conceited, lovers of pleasure
rather than lovers of God.

— 2 Timothy 3:1–4

NOTICE FROM THE DEVOTIONAL PASSAGE above that the
conditions delineated by the Apostle Paul seem to describe
our present world fairly accurately. Just watch television, read
a few magazines, catch the news or rent a movie and you will
see these attitudes and practices displayed. A skeptic might
challenge: "Are these behaviors only characteristic of our age?"
Obviously not. But increasingly they picture what is accepted
as normative in our culture.

This reality leads some moralists into lament and withdrawal. But for Christ followers, these challenges present an opportunity for a wider harvest! In reality, effective ministry can flourish in all societal contexts. In fact, an expansion of the Church has often occurred during times of change, difficulty and even persecution.

To his friends in Corinth Paul related that "a great door for effective work has opened to me" (1 Corinthians 16:9a). To the church at Colossae he requested: "Pray for us, too, that God may open a door for our message, so that we may proclaim the mystery of Christ, for which I am in chains" (Colossians 4:3). In Jesus' letters to the seven churches in the Revelation our Lord affirmed: "These are the words of him who is holy and true, who holds the key of David. What he opens no one can shut, and what he shuts no one can open. I know your deeds. See, I have placed before you an open door that no one can shut" (Revelation 3:7, 8).

What might an *open door* look like in our culture? Futurists predict that the United States will face greater cultural diversity, deeper economic volatility, weaker personal morality and broader insecurity. Demographically, America's singles population will continue to grow. Adoptive families, single-parent families and blended families will increase. The colorization of America will also continue as former *minorities* collectively become the new majority. Urbanization will increase. The disparity between rich and poor will widen. Illiteracy will become rampant among city youth. America will continue to mature as Boomers move into retirement. Bio-ethical debates about quality of life will cause tension between the young and old, especially over the explosion of health care costs and economic uncertainties. In summary, the new world ahead will be one of growing complexity and challenge.

I believe that Jesus opens a door of opportunity for each of his followers. However, that door is formed in the shape of a cross. For our Lord also taught: "Whoever wants to be my disciples must deny themselves and take up their cross and follow me" (Matthew 16:24). Fear keeps us from opening the door to see what is on the other side. Faith walks us through the door to embrace new opportunities. When Christians walk through the door of self denial, they emerge into a field of dreams.

I am not sure what conditions face your ministry today, or what challenges your team will experience in the days ahead. But irrespective of context, the Lord's invitation remains: "I tell you, open your eyes and look at the fields! They are ripe for harvest" (John 4:35b).

Group Exercise:

Identify some ministry opportunities disguised as challenges.

Should your team look further into moving through one of these doors?

Team Prayer:

Father, thank You for inviting us into your service. Forgive us for not accepting invitations

to ministry which you have placed before us.
Please lift our eyes to the harvest, so that as you
lead, we will walk through the doors that you
open. Amen!

Final Thought:

We are all faced with a series of great
opportunities brilliantly disguised as impossible
situations.

— Chuck Swindoll

Community

Therefore, brothers and sisters, since we have
confidence to enter the Most Holy Place by the
blood of Jesus, by a new and living way opened
for us through the curtain, that is, his body, and
since we have a great priest over the house of
God, let us draw near to God with a sincere heart
in full assurance of faith, having our hearts
sprinkled to cleanse us from a guilty conscience
and having our bodies washed with pure water.
Let us hold unswervingly to the hope we profess,
for he who promised is faithful. And let us
consider how we may spur one another on toward
love and good deeds, not giving up meeting
together, as some are in the habit of doing, but
encouraging one another— and all the more as
you see the Day approaching.
— Hebrews 10:19–25

WHY DO YOU THINK PEOPLE go to bars, join clubs or participate
in on-line communities? When asked, they tell us it's because

they want to connect with others. They desire friendship and companionship. They want to know, and to be known, preferably in a safe environment. But too often people are looking for love in all the wrong places.

Each one of us has an image of ourselves. That picture is a composite created by the feedback we receive from others. We feel good about ourselves when we are wanted, accepted and praised. Conversely, we feel badly about ourselves when we are ignored, rejected or demeaned. The stories of those who have lived up or down to people's expectations are numerous.

God knows that humanity has this need for fellowship. He made us this way. That's why He tells us that we are loved; that's why He adopts us into His family; and that's why He wants us to belong to a Christian community.

Many people view the church as a building, or as an event that takes place on Sunday mornings. We hear comments like, "I left my Bible at church," or, "I think I'll go to church tomorrow," which are understandable, but mask the truth. For the Bible is explicit in its revelation that the Church is people. It is believers called into a new community. And it is in this community that they discover acceptance and encouragement, and find faith, hope and love.

The text above makes it clear that the pursuit of community must be intentional, and the verses below point out how God expects His children to live together:

- ◆ Let us draw near to God (v. 22).

- ◆ Let us hold unswervingly to the hope we profess (v. 23).

- ◆ Let us consider how to spur one another on to love (v.24).

- ◆ Let us not give up meeting together (v. 25).
- ◆ Let us encourage one another (v. 25).

These admonitions, along with more than a dozen *one anothers* in the New Testament, make it clear that Christian fellowship is not an option. God knows that in community we become what we cannot become by ourselves. In community we know and are known. We do not lose our identity in community; we find it.

I [John] once had a conversation with a young man in Boulder, Colorado, who asserted: "I don't need to go to church to worship God; I can worship God out here on the Flat Irons." I agreed that this was possible, yet countered: "True, but you can't become all that God wants you to be apart from Christian community. For this is his vehicle for your nurture and the exercising of your gifts to others." The bottom line is that doing life together is God's design for humanity.

As leaders, let's never be satisfied by how many people are attending our events. Let's look deeper and ask how many are involved in Christian community. And as team leaders, don't limit your time together solely in program accomplishments— also enjoy your relationship together as friends.

Group Exercise:

What are some ways you can build community among your team?

Plan an activity together, outside of your service responsibility, that will help you to get to know one another better.

Team Prayer:

Father, we confess that we live fairly private lives. And though we attend activities together, we have not become truly devoted to one another. We know the pain of carrying burdens alone, and see the great need for community in our lives. Therefore we ask You, dear Lord, to use us to connect people to one another through this ministry. Amen!

Final Thought:

What I am at any given moment in the process of my becoming a person will be determined by my relationships with those who love me or refuse to love me, with those I love or refuse to love.

— John Powell

Prayer

And when you pray, do not be like the hypocrites,
for they love to pray standing in the synagogues
and on the street corners to be seen by others.
Truly I tell you, they have received their reward in
full. But when you pray, go into your room, close
the door and pray to your Father, who is unseen.
Then your Father, who sees what is done in secret,
will reward you. And when you pray, do not keep
on babbling like pagans, for they think they will
be heard because of their many words. Do not be
like them, for your Father knows what you need
before you ask him. This, then, is how you should
pray: 'Our Father in heaven, hallowed be your
name, your kingdom come, your will be done,
on earth as it is in heaven. Give us today our
daily bread. And forgive us our debts, as we also
have forgiven our debtors. And lead us not into
temptation, but deliver us from the evil one.'

— **Matthew 6:5–13**

WE HAVE ALL HEARD THE expression: "When all else fails, pray." But this wasn't Jesus' attitude. For Him prayer was a way of life (see, for example, Luke 3:21; 4:42; 5:16 and 6:12). He enjoyed communion with His Father (John 17:4). He shared personal concerns that were on His heart (Luke 22:42). And He interceded for His friends (John 17:15). You would think that if anyone wouldn't need prayer, it would be the eternal Son, since He was already connected to the Father. Yet Jesus regularly prayed.

Prayer is essential for:

- Eternal life (Romans 10:13)
- Maintaining fellowship (1 John 1:9)
- Effective witness (Matthew 9:38)
- Resisting temptation (Matthew 14:38)
- Daily guidance (Proverbs 3:5 & 6)

Prayer is not as much a discipline as it is a dialog. It is communion, communication and affection in words. It's not trying to squeeze some answer out of God. It's about enjoying His presence. Healthy families communicate regularly. Likewise in our conversations with the Father, all joys, concerns and hopes can be expressed daily.

We don't change God's mind through prayer. He already has our best interest at heart. Rather in the words of Charles Finney: "Prayer produces such an effect in us as renders it consistent for God to do in us that which He wanted to do even before we prayed." Like the Son, we come to the Father saying, not my will, but Your will be done (see Luke 22:42b).

Some people teach a "name it and claim it" view of prayer based on a lopsided understanding of Mark 11:24. They boldly demand God to answer their petitions according to their own expected outcomes. However, even Jesus did not do this. Likewise, the Apostle Paul, after repeated requests, only heard, "My grace is sufficient for you" (2 Corinthians 12:7–10).

A balanced view of intercession encourages us to take our requests to God, but then to let Him determine the best response. "Do not be anxious about anything, but in everything, by prayer and petition, with thanksgiving, present your request to God. And the peace of God, which transcends all understanding, will guard your hearts and minds in Christ Jesus" (Philippians 4:6, 7).

From our finite viewpoint we don't know what's best in a given situation. But as we honestly share our concerns, the Lord's peace guards our thoughts and emotions, irrespective of the outcome. Truly this is our deepest need.

As members of a ministry team, never reduce prayer to an opening exercise at a meeting or program event. Rather, as individuals and as a team, enjoy rich times of communion with God.

Group Exercise:

What is one area where you can use the peace of Christ right now?

Team Prayer:

Oh Father, thank You for the privilege of calling You Father. Thank You for Your deep love and for Your open invitation to commune with You often. We praise You for Your Son who prays for us, and for Your Holy Spirit who intercedes for us when we don't even know how to pray. May You receive much glory through the people drawn to You thorough this ministry. Thy Kingdom come; Thy will be done. Amen!

Final Thought:

It's impossible to walk the talk, unless we continually talk the walk!

Balance

When Joseph and Mary had done everything
required by the Law of the Lord, they returned
to Galilee to their own town of Nazareth. And
the child grew and became strong; he was filled
with wisdom, and the grace of God was on him.

Every year Jesus' parents went to Jerusalem
for the Festival of the Passover. When he was
twelve years old, they went up to the Festival,
according to the custom. After the Festival was
over, while his parents were returning home, the
boy Jesus stayed behind in Jerusalem, but they
were unaware of it. Thinking he was in their
company, they traveled on for a day. Then they
began looking for him among their relatives
and friends. When they did not find him, they
went back to Jerusalem to look for him. After
three days they found him in the temple courts,
sitting among the teachers, listening to them
and asking them questions. Everyone who heard
him was amazed at his understanding and his

answers. When his parents saw him, they were
astonished. His mother said to him, 'Son, why
have you treated us like this? Your father and I
have been anxiously searching for you.' 'Why
were you searching for me?' He asked. 'Didn't
you know I had to be in my Father's house?' But
they did not understand what he was saying
to them. Then he went down to Nazareth with
them and was obedient to them. But his mother
treasured all these things in her heart. And as
Jesus grew up, he increased in wisdom and in
favor with God and people.

— Luke 2:39–52

WHEN I [FRED] WAS A college student, I taught a Sunday school class every week at the Maxwell Street YMCA in Chicago. After class, we'd check out the merchandise in the street market and watch the many characters doing their thing.

One Sunday a disheveled man pushed his way through the crowd and stopped right in front of me. He pointed his finger at the Bible under my arm and said: "You don't believe that, do you?" "Yes, I do," I replied. "Nobody believes that," he snarled. "Everybody knows that Jesus was kidnapped for 18 years." I stood dumbfounded as the stranger disappeared through the crowd.

His comment irritated me and caused me to do some research when I returned home. Was there any validity to his absurd remark? Searching the scriptures, I could find no description of the life of Christ from the time He was 12 years old until He was a man of 30. Had the indigent man known what he was talking about?

I finally discovered one verse that described the life of Christ during the 18 years of preparation for His public ministry. This period of time in His life has been referred to as the silent years. In chapter two, verse 52, Luke summarized the four areas of activity that characterize the life of Christ— "And as Jesus grew up, he increased in wisdom and in favor with God and people." Jesus Christ had a balanced life.

Effective leadership requires living a balanced life— growing physically, intellectually, spiritually and socially. An over-emphasis or lack of emphasis in any of these areas will cause problems. For example, when we are physically ill or out of shape, we lose the stamina to do that which needs to be done. Relational problems can lead to irritation, withdrawal, lack of sleep, overeating or no appetite at all. When we are lonely or fatigued, we are more vulnerable spiritually. When we have been neglecting spiritual disciplines, we are less sensitive to others. And we can keep connecting the dots. Holistic self care requires balanced attendance to the various dimensions of our lives.

As a leader your personal well-being is determined by the degree to which you maintain balance in these four dimensions of life. But God never intended for His people to go it alone in these practices. As members of a team you can look out for one another. Share spiritual challenges and prayer requests. Pass on insights or advice that you have learned. Hold each other accountable to get in shape. And encourage one another regularly. In turn, your ministry together will honor God and bless others.

Group Exercise:

Each team member share a response to the statement: This is what I can do to bring greater balance in my life.

Team Prayer:

Heavenly Father, help us to take time to assess the activities in which we are involved. If our lives have gotten out of balance, assist us in making the necessary adjustments. Thank You for giving us Jesus as our example and our guide. And thank You for giving us one another as encouragers in our journey. Amen!

Final Thought:

The Christian walk requires a transfer of balance as we move from one step to the next.

Failure

Afterward Jesus appeared again to his disciples,
by the Sea of Galilee. It happened this way:
Simon Peter, Thomas (also known as Didymus),
Nathanael from Cana in Galilee, the sons of
Zebedee, and two other disciples were together. 'I'm
going out to fish,' Simon Peter told them, and
they said, 'We'll go with you.' So they went out
and got into the boat, but that night they caught
nothing. Early in the morning, Jesus stood on
the shore, but the disciples did not realize that
it was Jesus. He called out to them, 'Friends,
haven't you any fish?' 'No,' they answered. He
said, 'Throw your net on the right side of the boat
and you will find some.' When they did, they
were unable to haul the net in because of the large
number of fish.

—John 21:1–6

PETER HAD GREAT PLANS FOR the future. Not only did he look
forward to being part of the coming Kingdom, he aspired for a

place next to the Lord. In the span of a few short days, however, Peter's hopes and dreams collapsed. During the events leading up to the crucifixion, he had refused to be identified as one of the Lord's disciples. On three separate occasions he lacked courage to take a stand in a hostile environment.

Having failed in his relationship with the Master, Peter went back to the profession in which he had previously experienced success. Early one morning he and his buddies embarked on a fishing excursion. Although they were familiar with the best fishing spots on the lake, they headed back toward the shore, frustrated with an empty catch.

This probably was not the first time they had been skunked, but the circumstances on this occasion were different. It came in the midst of the most discouraging time in Peter's life.

To make matters worse, someone on the shore had witnessed their failure. "Catch anything?" Usually there were plenty of excuses on the tip of Peter's tongue. Excuses such as it was too windy, or the water was too warm, would have been adequate responses. But their reply to this pointed question was simply, "No." They were tired, confused and discouraged.

We, too, have moments like Peter had. And if we are teachable, we can experience transformational growth. On that beach Peter was renewed, reinstated and recharged for ministry. The love of Christ and the power of His resurrection is more than enough to handle any failure that we may encounter.

Think of all the biblical leaders who became successful after experiencing failure. Look, for example, at the lives of Abraham, Moses, Elijah, David and Paul. A reality of life is that leaders don't hit the mark every time. This is not making excuses; it is just true. And our failures, while embarrassing to us (and at times to our friends), hurt most deeply because we feel we have disappointed God, whom we love dearly.

But notice from the account in John 21 that hope is always near by when Jesus is present. When Peter was moving in the wrong direction, Jesus gave him, and He gives us, some practical steps to change failure into a blessing:

- ◆ Admit our failure (21:3–5)
- ◆ Listen to biblical advice (21:6a)
- ◆ Obey the Lord's direction (21:6b)
- ◆ Seek restoration (21:7–14)
- ◆ Establish new priorities (21:15–19)
- ◆ Cease comparison with others (21:20–22)

Because of his failure, Peter was ready to resign his position as a spokesman for the Lord. But this was not Christ's desire for him. Instead, the Lord invited Peter and the other disciples into a future filled with great ministry opportunities.

Likewise, we may be tempted to resign our leadership position in the wake of failure. In fact, Satan, called the Accuser, would love to see us remain on the sidelines after a fall. But Christ already paid the penalty for our sin, and He encourages us to keep moving on. By following the steps above, as individuals and as a team, we can renew our spiritual service.

Group Exercise:

When you've dropped the ball, what has hindered your recovery?

What has helped your recovery?

Team Prayer:

Lord, as we look back on our lives as Christians and now as leaders, many things haven't turned out the way we expected. We know we have disappointed You, and at times hurt those around us. Thank You for Your forgiveness. And thank You that You still want to use us as leaders in ministry. Help us to view failures as possible stepping stones to new opportunities for service in Your Kingdom. Amen!

Final Thought:

Success is never final; failure is never fatal.

— **Winston Churchill**

Expectations

Because of the LORD's great love we are not
consumed, for his compassions never fail.
They are new every morning; great is your
faithfulness. I say to myself, 'The LORD is my
portion; therefore I will wait for him.' The LORD
is good to those whose hope is in him, to the one
who seeks him; it is good to wait quietly for the
salvation of the LORD.

— Lamentations 3:22–26

SOMEONE ASKED A COLLEGE FOOTBALL player who had recently
become a Christian to explain the main difference in his
life before and after his conversion. "When I woke up in the
morning my first words used to be: 'Good god, morning!' Now
when I awake my first words are 'Good morning, God!'"

Notice how a similar optimism and enthusiasm flow from
this devotional passage. Amidst challenging times, the writer
of Lamentations declares that God is greater than his problems.

God is compassionate and good to those who hope and seek Him. God's goodness is so great that each morning the writer anticipates waking up awed by His mercies.

Are you expecting something good to happen today? I hope so, because this could be the best day of your life. Take a moment to read these inspiring words:

Today, when I awoke, I suddenly realized that this is the best day of my life, ever! There were times when I wondered if I would make it to today, but I did! And because I did I'm going to celebrate!

Today, I'm going to celebrate what an unbelievable life I have had so far: the accomplishments, the many blessings, and, yes, even the hardships because they have served to make me stronger.

I will go through this day with a happy heart, and my head held high. I will marvel at God's seemingly simple gifts: the morning dew, the sun, the clouds, the trees, the flowers, the birds.

Today, none of these miraculous creations will escape my notice.

Today, I will share my excitement for life with other people. Today is the day I quit worrying about what I don't have and start being grateful for all the wonderful things God has already given me.

And tonight, before I go to bed, I'll go outside and raise my eyes to the heavens. I will stand in awe at the beauty of the stars and the moon, and I will praise God for these magnificent treasures.

As the day ends and I lay my head on my pillow, I will thank the Almighty for the best day of my life. And I will sleep the sleep of a contented child, excited with expectation because I know tomorrow is going to be the best day of my life, ever! — Anonymous

What an outlook on life! Don't you wish you could meet the author? This writer gets it. No doubt, she or he would affirm the admonishment of Paul who declared: "Rejoice in the Lord always. I will say it again: Rejoice!" (Philippians 4:4).

Evangelist Merv Rosell often began his day by praying: "Lord, what's happening in Your world today and how do I get in on it?" May we likewise, as individuals and as a team, anticipate great days ahead because of the greatness of the Creator of our days!

Group Exercise:

Describe a time when either a positive or negative expectation led to its realization.

Team Prayer:

Thank You, Heavenly Father for this day. We look forward to Your leading in our lives and in this ministry. We ask that You use this meeting for our growth and Your glory. Amen!

Final Thought:

Attempt great things for God and expect great things from God.

— William Carey

Forgiveness

Then Peter came to Jesus and asked, 'Lord, how many times shall I forgive someone who sins against me? Up to seven times?' Jesus answered, 'I tell you, not seven times, but seventy-seven times. Therefore, the kingdom of heaven is like a king who wanted to settle accounts with his servants. As he began the settlement, a man who owed him ten thousand bags of gold was brought to him. Since he was not able to pay, the master ordered that he and his wife and his children and all that he had be sold to repay the debt. The servant fell on his knees before him. 'Be patient with me,' he begged, 'and I will pay back everything.' The servant's master took pity on him, canceled the debt and let him go. But when that servant went out, he found one of his fellow servants who owed him a hundred silver coins. He grabbed him and began to choke him. 'Pay back what you owe me!' he demanded. His fellow servant fell to his knees and begged him, 'Be patient with me, and I will pay you back.' But he refused. Instead, he went off and had the man thrown into prison until he could pay the debt. When the other servants saw what had happened, they were greatly distressed and went and told their master everything that had happened. Then the master called the servant in. 'You wicked servant,' he said, 'I canceled all that debt of yours because you begged me to. Shouldn't you have had mercy on your fellow servant just as I had on you?' In anger his master handed him over to the jailers to be tortured, until he should pay back all he owed. This is how My heavenly Father will treat each of you unless you forgive a brother or sister from your heart.'

— Matthew 18:21–35

DON'T YOU JUST LOVE PETER? With him, what you see is what you get. He knows he doesn't have his act together, but he loves Christ deeply, and wants to be more like Him.

On this occasion he asked Jesus: "Lord, just how far do we have to take this forgiveness thing?" Most likely this wasn't a philosophical exercise for the big fisherman. He was probably irritated with someone and wanted the straight stuff from Jesus. And his offer of seven times implies that he was really trying.

But Jesus responds: "Not seven times, but seventy times seven." He tells Peter (along with the disciples gathered there, and all of us reading the account today) that we are never in a position to withhold forgiveness. We must always be quick to forgive. Even in the most difficult of situations, we can choose to embody and display God's love and acceptance. We can offer one another the peace and freedom of a cleared conscience and a restored relationship.

Our Lord explained this, as He frequently did, by telling a story. Through this parable Jesus painted a picture of God's mercy, and His expectation that His children act mercifully. Since our heavenly Father has forgiven us such a HUGE debt, we should likewise forgive those who have sinned against us. We, who have been graced, should be gracious.

As we receive God's love, we sense a deep obligation to pass on forgiveness. Therefore, let us meditate on the following words from the Psalms, and open our hearts to likewise forgive.

> The Lord is compassionate and gracious, slow to anger and abounding in love. He will not always accuse, nor will he harbor his anger forever; he does not treat us as our sins deserve or repay us according to our iniquities. For as high as the heavens are above the earth, so great is his love for those who fear him; as far as the east is from the west, so far has he removed our transgressions from us (103:8–12).

God has designed us to live in community. We grow and mature through interaction with one another. But since all of us are imperfect people, we also offend one another from time to time. Therefore God requires that we are also quick to forgive one another. Whether forgiveness is needed toward a team member or someone we serve, it provides the healing balm essential to relational unity.

Group Exercise:

In pairs, confidentially share a situation that requires more mercy from you toward another. Pray for each other.

Team Prayer:

Father, as we come to You now, we remember the words of the Publican, who prayed, 'Lord, be merciful unto me, a sinner,' and we admit that we are but the same. Yet we also know Your forgiveness— so undeserved and so lavished upon us. Therefore, we ask You to make us instruments of Your mercy to others, so that which we have freely received, we would freely give. Amen!

Final Thought:

Bitterness poisons the vessel in which it is held.

Generosity

Command those who are rich in this present world
not to be arrogant nor to put their hope in wealth,
which is so uncertain, but to put their hope in
God, who richly provides us with everything for
our enjoyment. Command them to do good, to
be rich in good deeds, and to be generous and
willing to share. In this way they will lay up
treasure for themselves as a firm foundation for
the coming age, so that they may take hold of
the life that is truly life.

— 1 Timothy 6:17–19

WE HAVE ALL HEARD THE expression, "use it, or lose it!" Muscles atrophy, skills decline and resources depreciate. Whether we're an athlete, surgeon or businessperson, regular practice in our profession is essential for continual effectiveness.

Likewise, generosity is also a skill that is maximized through routine practice. Lives are influenced when resources are released to meet needs. Therefore, it should not surprise us that the Bible admonishes leaders to keep a right perspective on money.

In this passage Paul is not warning against having money, or even having too much money. The apostle tells us that God "provides us with everything for our enjoyment" (v. 17). God assumes that we will use resources for our personal well being. A miserly, self-denigrating lifestyle is not more spiritual than a comfortable, appreciative lifestyle. Christ followers are free to enjoy a round of golf, eat a fine meal or sleep in a comfortable bed.

However, leaders <u>are</u> charged not to become *arrogant* because of their wealth. The world highly values money, so people with means may be tempted to measure their value according to their portfolio. Even more problematic is the possibility that the prosperous may begin to think their resources can safeguard their future. The truth, however, is that riches are uncertain. Only God is dependably constant.

God is not impressed with the amount of money we have in our bank accounts or 401(k) retirement plans. In fact, the more we place our trust in these resources, the more we disappoint Him. The Lord delights in those who value what He values—and money, as a value, is not on His list.

Working hard, saving and investing are important. But we dare not become prideful over our accumulation. Money itself is not the end; it is a means. God is interested in what we do with our resources. Wealth gives us a capacity to increase our distribution.

God condemns the self-indulgent person who hoards rather than shares. And He blesses and calls *rich* those who are generous (v. 18). Generosity drives out greed. We can never become ensnared by a resource that we freely give away.

Therefore, as long as we are willing to share our resources with others, we are also free to enjoy from the bounty that the Lord has entrusted to us. Furthermore, all treasure that we invest in Kingdom enterprises today is escrowed into eternity. Deeds of grace and acts of generosity offered now become "a firm foundation for the coming age" (v.19).

As Christ followers and servant leaders, look for ways to expand your generosity. Perhaps you could babysit for the children of others while they are serving. Perhaps your team may collect a gift to financially assist another ministry. Or perhaps you may underwrite a project together. Anything that expands your capacity for generosity, deepens your Christian walk and edifies those you serve.

Group Exercise:

Choose a team generosity project— such as those in the examples above. Decide the when, where and how required for an appropriate action step.

Team Prayer:

Father, we acknowledge that every blessing that we have comes from Your gracious hand. Even our ability to earn an income is provided by You in the way You designed us. So we thank you for Your goodness. And above all we thank You for the priceless gift of Your Son. Increase our generosity for Your Kingdom's sake and for Your glory. This we humbly pray through Jesus Christ our Lord. Amen!

Final Thought:

True wealth is not measured by accumulation but by distribution.

God's Will

Now we ask you, brothers and sisters, to acknowledge those who work hard among you, who care for you in the Lord and who admonish you. Hold them in the highest regard in love because of their work. Live in peace with each other. And we urge you, brothers and sisters, warn those who are idle and disruptive, encourage the disheartened, help the weak, be patient with everyone. Make sure that nobody pays back wrong for wrong, but always strive to do what is good for each other and for everyone else. Rejoice always, pray continually, give thanks in all circumstances; for this is God's will for you in Christ Jesus. Do not put out the Spirit's fire. Do not treat prophecies with contempt but test them all; hold on to what is good, reject whatever is harmful.

— 1 Thessalonians 5:12–22

IT WAS TIME FOR THE new church I [Fred] was serving to officially organize. One of the important steps in the process was to call a Recognition Council. Delegates from sister churches came to examine such items as our membership, history and constitution.

In our constitution we had chosen to call the church officers, *deacons* and *trustees*. When the Recognition Council came to the section on church offices, one delegate asked: "Where do you find trustees in the Bible?"

His question was followed by an awkward silence. I knew I had no answer to his question. There were no trustees in the Bible. Another pastor came to my rescue: "You'll find trustees in the same verse where you'll find the clerk and the treasurer," he replied. After everyone had a good laugh, the discussion shifted to another topic.

Since that night I have often reflected on that brief interchange. Christians believe the Bible is our final rule of faith and practice. However, the Bible is not always prescriptive. As in the matter of church government, it may be descriptive. Therefore, we need to distinguish between what the early church did and what we should do.

The Bible does not give us an exhaustive list of God's will on each item for which we must make decisions. It is true that in some things God is definitive. We read for example: "What I have purposed I have purposed" (Isaiah 14:24). Some things God has decided, and they are immutable.

And it is clear from the devotional passage above that certain attitudes and practices are always God's will. God is always honored when we are patient with others and are peacemakers. He is pleased when we continually talk with Him, when we are joyful and appreciative. These behaviors are always His will.

Interestingly, one thing that God has willed, however, is that in many things He allows us choice. For example, in the Book of Acts we read: "It seemed good to the Holy Spirit and us not to burden you with anything beyond the following requirements ...." The Jerusalem counsel did not have specific scripture on which Hebraic practices Gentile Christians should follow. But as they discussed it together, and sensed God's Spirit leading them, they came to a conclusion that made sense to them.

As members of a ministry team, you have God's precepts to instruct you, the Holy Spirit to guide you, and the common sense He has given each of you to serve in creative, God honoring ways. Seek first to honor God, and the decisions of life become clearer.

Group Exercise:

Read Philippians 4:8 and agree to memorize this values template. At your next meeting, take turns quoting this scripture.

Team Prayer:

Dear Lord, Thank You for Your Word. May we use it as our guide as we make decisions. Although we may not always find specific instructions, may we use our Spirit-controlled minds to make the best decisions. Amen!

Final Thought:

Love God, and live as you please!

— **Augustine**

Anger

Saul's anger flared up at Jonathan and he said to him, 'You son of a perverse and rebellious woman! Don't I know that you have sided with the son of Jesse to your own shame and to the shame of the mother who bore you? As long as the son of Jesse lives on this earth, neither you nor your kingdom will be established. Now send someone to bring him to me, for he must die!' 'Why should he be put to death? What has he done?' Jonathan asked his father. But Saul hurled his spear at him to kill him. Then Jonathan knew that his father intended to kill David. Jonathan got up from the table in fierce anger; on that second day of the feast he did not eat, because he was grieved at his father's shameful treatment of David.

— 1 Samuel 20:30–34

WOW— TALK ABOUT A FAMILY argument! The anger level at this family meal is so high that in his rage the father swears at his son and tries to kill him. And in his anger, the son storms out of the house.

We might think, well, this was King Saul, thousands of years ago, and he wasn't too spiritual. This couldn't happen today, right? Hopefully, this level of anger would never erupt in our homes and in ministry. But reality tells us that the potential for anger and frustration exists in all relationships.

A number of years ago I [John] had a friend serving in a particularly challenging ministry. Frequently he would say, "I'm really frustrated," and then go on to tell me what was troubling him. After a series of such comments, I looked at him and said: "Hey, admit it, you're not frustrated, you're really angry." He looked at me seriously; paused; and then admitted with a sheepish smile: "Yeah, I really am."

Anger is hard to admit. It seems more spiritual to say we are troubled, hurt, offended, annoyed, sore, irritated or frustrated. Nevertheless, the basic emotion is the same. One psychologist defines anger like this: "By anger we mean that feeling of tension and aggressiveness which arises in a person when they face a frustrating obstacle or another individual who is a threat to some cherished value like self-esteem" (Vernon Grounds). When our ideas, preferences or identity are thwarted, an emotional energy is released within us.

Now it is interesting to note that the emotion of frustration and anger is by itself not sin. To feel this is to be human. In the Bible we read: "In your anger do not sin" (Ephesians 4:26a). Sin only results when this emotion is not properly handled.

Two harmful ways of dealing with this emotional arousal are blowing up and clamming up. Obviously, verbally or physically assaulting the source of our frustration is damaging.

Less obvious, but equally harmful, is stuffing this authentic emotion. Anger suppressed can lead to bitterness, hatred, loathing, withdrawal, depression, high blood pressure, colitis, ulcers and heart disease. Not a good way to handle anger!

The healthy way to deal with anger involves a three step process. First, we need to talk with the Lord about those things which frustrate us. In the Psalms, for example, David pours out to the Lord his wounds, vexations and fury. And remember, God invites us to talk to Him about anything that troubles us (Philippians 4:6).

Second, God tells us to release that anger by forgiving the source of our irritations. In fact, we are to forgive in the same way that the Lord has forgiven us (Colossians. 3:13). This releasing is so important that Jesus warned: "For if you forgive men when they sin against you, your Heavenly Father will also forgive you. But if you do not forgive men their sins, your Father will not forgive your sins" (Matthew 6:14, 15).

Third, we should talk with the person about the irritating incident. Earlier we read the admonition: "in your anger do not sin" (Ephesians 4:26a). This verse continues: "Do not let the sun go down while you are still angry, and do not give the devil a foothold" (4:26b, 27). In other words, while the emotion is real, we do not have to sin. We can avoid the destruction of silent bitterness or damaging words. But as soon as possible, perhaps after we have calmed down a bit, we need to talk to the person. And the Scriptures provide advice on how to express our concern:

- ◆ Speak privately (Matthew 18:15)
- ◆ Speak softly (Proverbs 15:1)
- ◆ Speak carefully (Proverbs 21:23)

- ◆ Speak intentionally (Proverbs 12:15, 16)
- ◆ Speak specifically (Ephesians 4:15)
- ◆ Speak graciously (Proverbs 22:11)

As members of a ministry team, *when* you come to moments of frustration with one another or with someone to whom you minister (notice I didn't say *if*), use that emotional energy of anger to bring clarity of mission and growth in relationship.

Group Exercise:

On the blow up—clam up continuum, toward which direction are you most likely to err?

What has been beneficial for you in handling relational anger?

Team Prayer:

Lord Jesus, we pray in the words You taught us, 'forgive us our trespasses, as we forgive those who trespass against us.' We want to honor You in our hearts and in our words. So when we sense annoyance and irritation, stir us to healthy resolve in order to honor You and encourage one another. Amen!

Final Thought:

Instead of just counting to 10 when angry, ask yourself, 'What will my anger accomplish?' Then with a list of harmful consequences in mind, ask the Lord, 'Where do we go from here?'

Interruptions

As soon as they left the synagogue, they went
with James and John to the home of Simon and
Andrew. Simon's mother-in-law was in bed
with a fever, and they immediately told Jesus
about her. So He went to her, took her hand and
helped her up. The fever left her and she began
to wait on them. That evening after sunset the
people brought to Jesus all the sick and demon-
possessed. The whole town gathered at the door,
and Jesus healed many who had various diseases.
He also drove out many demons, but he would
not let the demons speak because they knew who
he was. Very early in the morning, while it was
still dark, Jesus got up, left the house and went
off to a solitary place, where he prayed. Simon
and his companions went to look for him, and
when they found him, they exclaimed: 'Everyone
is looking for you!' Jesus replied, 'Let us go
somewhere else— to the nearby villages— so I can
preach there also. That is why I have come.' So he

traveled throughout Galilee, preaching in their synagogues and driving out demons.

— Mark 1:29–39

WOULDN'T IT HAVE BEEN GREAT to live during the days of Jesus when the pace of life was more relaxed? When daily activities were less complicated and interruptions were far fewer? People in the first century didn't seem to have many of the pressures we face today.

A look at the life of Jesus, however, reveals that daily demands were always present. As a leader, Jesus was extremely busy, and His planned activities were constantly being interrupted.

Take a look, for example, at just one day in His life as recorded in Mark 1. Jesus began this day teaching on the Sabbath in a synagogue (21, 22). During the middle of His teaching a man with an evil spirit interrupted Him. Jesus stopped His teaching and exorcised the evil spirit (23–25).

After the synagogue service Jesus went to the home of Simon and Andrew. This should have been a well-deserved time to relax. But Simon's mother-in-law was in bed with a fever. So Jesus took time to heal her (29–31).

That same day, after sunset, people brought the sick and demon-possessed to Him to be healed. According to Scripture, the whole town gathered at the door, and He healed many of them (32–34).

Very early the next morning while it was still dark, Jesus arose early to pray. He found a place where He would be unheard, unobserved and undisturbed. One would think that if He started early enough in a secluded enough place, He would be able to avoid interruptions. Yet, Peter and his friends found Him. "Everyone is looking for you," they exclaimed.

Notice how Jesus responded to their interruption. No rebuke. No ignoring their intrusion. He simply decided: "Let's go somewhere else— to the nearby villages— so I can preach there also. That is why I have come" (v. 38).

Personally, I [Fred] don't like interruptions. They seem like an invasion by the enemy to divert me from accomplishing my ministry goals. But years ago a friend helped me gain a better perspective on interruptions. At the beginning of a meeting he prayed, "Lord, help us to understand that the interruptions to our ministry may be our ministry."

What a provocative biblical insight! In reality, we cannot schedule ministry like we schedule appointments. Many ministry opportunities come at inconvenient times. People have often expressed being influenced more through an informal moment than during a program. Our presence, at just the right time, when someone is hurting, can deepen their relationship with Christ and with us.

So as we ask God to control our agendas this day, let's also welcome the ministry opportunities that He disguises as interruptions.

Group Exercise:

Describe a situation where an interruption became a divine appointment.

Team Prayer:

All knowing God, You know how full our agenda is today. May we be disciplined enough to complete it, yet flexible enough to be sensitive to the needs of others. May we realize that the interruptions to our ministry may be our ministry. Amen!

Final Thought:

Interruptions can be viewed as sources of irritation or opportunities for service, as moments lost or experiences gained, as time wasted or horizons gained.

— William A. Ward

The Journey

I have fought the good fight, I have finished the
race, I have kept the faith. Now there is in store for
me the crown of righteousness, which the Lord,
the righteous Judge, will award to me on that
day— and not only to me, but also to all who
have longed for his appearing.

— 2 Timothy 4:7–8

A MINNESOTA FRIEND OF MINE tells a story of his irritation with traveling through the state of Wisconsin. Because of business and family in Chicago, he traveled through the dairy state several times each year. For him, Wisconsin was always a place just to get through as quickly as possible. But on one trip he noticed how beautiful Wisconsin really is. And he had to admit that in his typical rush to destination, he had been missing the beauty of the journey.

This rush to destination doesn't just take place on highways. An end-product focus is tempting to worship teams planning a weekend event, youth leaders working on a student retreat and teachers rushing through lesson material.

Admittedly, destination *is* important. Knowing our destination informs our journey. And results do matter. The Bible records, for example, the occasions and numbers of people coming to Christ. But numbers are not the bottom line. Scripture also records the personal stories of many of these converts.

The Apostle Paul serves as a good model of balancing task and relationship. Paul was definitely results oriented. He moved from town to town with a passion of introducing more people to Christ. But throughout his journey (more specifically, his three missionary journeys), he savored his time with people. New converts were not just numbers to him. He considered those he led to Christ as his children. His relationship with Philemon, for example, is so close that he could ask him to forgive a servant that had stolen from him. His friendship with Timothy was so deep that he called him his son. And his fellowship with Luke was so rich that the doctor remained with him until his death.

Our Lord Jesus provides the perfect example of balance between results and relationships. Frequently Jesus said— "I must." "I must go to Samaria" (John 4:4); "I must preach the Kingdom of God" (Luke 4:43); "I must go to Jerusalem" (Matthew 16:21); "I must press on today and tomorrow" (Luke 13:33). No one was more intentional and directional than Jesus.

Yet simultaneously, our Lord was highly relational. He enjoyed the company of friends (Mary, Martha and Lazarus), colleagues (the disciples) and even children. Jesus also had time for strangers like a Syrophenician woman, a seeking tax collector and a blind beggar.

As a ministry team, enjoy the journey! Avoid the peril of the either-or between results and relationships, progress and people. Individually, you are likely wired to be more relational or task oriented. But as a team, together, you can have both these orientations covered.

Enjoy your time together in prayer, in planning and in programs. Do keep your destination in mind, and do be results conscious, for those to whom we minister have eternal souls. Yet at the same time, slow down enough to hear the stories and deep concerns of those you serve. Be there for your family, for your friends and for one another. Amidst the press of service, savor the journey!

Group Exercise:

Is there an area where your team may have been so destination driven that you did not enjoy the journey as much as you might have preferred?

Team Prayer:

Father, we don't just want to sit around and enjoy Christian fellowship; we want to passionately make more disciples for Christ. But in our doing, let us not forget being. Help us to not be so program oriented that we fail to see people. Bring clarity to our destination, along with joy in the journey. Amen!

Final Thought:

When we mimic the gait of the Galilean, we notice what is important in ministry!

Love

Love must be sincere. Hate what is evil; cling to what is good. Be devoted to one another in love. Honor one another above yourselves. Never be lacking in zeal, but keep your spiritual fervor, serving the Lord. Be joyful in hope, patient in affliction, faithful in prayer. Share with the Lord's people who are in need. Practice hospitality. Bless those who persecute you; bless and do not curse. Rejoice with those who rejoice; mourn with those who mourn. Live in harmony with one another. Do not be proud, but be willing to associate with people of low position. Do not think you are superior. Do not repay anyone evil for evil. Be careful to do what is right in the eyes of everyone. If it is possible, as far as it depends on you, live at peace with everyone. Do not take revenge, my dear friends, but leave room for God's wrath, for it is written: 'It is mine

> to avenge; I will repay,' says the Lord. On the
> contrary: 'If your enemy is hungry, feed him;
> if he is thirsty, give him something to drink. In
> doing this, you will heap burning coals on his
> head.' Do not be overcome by evil, but overcome
> evil with good.
>
> — Romans 12:9–21

HOW'S YOUR LOVE LIFE? THE answer to this question will not
be discovered from an inventory in *People Magazine*. Rather the
creator of humanity, the author of love Himself, has provided
the criteria. Take a moment to review the following expressions
of love.

Love sincerely (v. 9).

    Let heartfelt affection be .... _____
expressed in helpful actions.

Cling to what is right (v. 9).

    Do only good to each other. .... _____

Be devoted (v. 10).

    Maintain the highest commitment .... _____
to others' well being.

Honor one another above yourself (v. 10).

    Esteem the worth and value of another. .... _____

Remain spiritually zealous by seizing opportunities (v. 11).

    Be intentional in demonstrating love............................ _____

Let hope keep you joyful (v. 12, NEB).

    Remain confident that people .... _____
can become new in Christ.

In your suffering be steadfast (v. 12).

Keep loving, even when it's.. _____
personally tough.

Maintain the habit of prayer (v. 12, Phillips).

Regularly ask God for his.. _____
best in the lives of others.

Provide generously for the needy (v. 13, Knox).

Give financial assistance to.. _____
the disadvantaged.

Practice hospitality (v. 13).

Let love be expressed in an .... _____
open home and shared resources.

Pray for those who hassle you (v. 14).

Don't just love those you like. .... _____
Love even the antagonist.

Be empathetic (v. 15).

Offer others a listening ear and .... _____
an understanding heart.

Live in harmony (vv. 16, 18).

Be willing to play a melodious .... _____
second fiddle.

Avoid snobbishness (v. 16).

Let love flow beyond your .... _____
particular in-group.

Do not retaliate (vv. 17, 19–21).

Lovingly let it go!.. _____

Now let's go back through the list and rank ourselves on each category using the following point scale:

Often (5 points)   Sometimes (3 points)   Rarely (1 point) Never (0 points)

Next, total up you point values, and see how you rank:

0 – 15 Points	Please don't tell anyone you are a Christ Follower!
15 – 30 Points	Let's start getting serious!
31 – 45 Points	You're getting warmer!
46 – 50 Points	People value your friendship!
51 – 65 Points	You're a great lover!
66 – 75 Points	Take the inventory again— this time truthfully! ☺

Obviously, we are all people in process! Learning to love is a lifelong journey. However, as we ponder the Father's love, follow the example of Jesus and respond to the Spirit's prompting, we can grow in this Christian practice. Those around us will benefit by our taking seriously the practice of love, and we will grow personally as we allow the love of Christ to flow through us.

Group Exercise:

In a circle response state which of the above expressions of love is the easiest or hardest for you.

Team Prayer:

Lord, make me an instrument of Thy peace.
Where there is hatred — let me sow love. Where
there is injury — pardon. Where there is
doubt — faith. Where there is despair —
hope. Where there is darkness — light. Where
there is sadness — joy. O Divine Master, grant
that I may not so much seek To be consoled — as
to console. To be understood — as to understand.
To be loved — as to love. For it is in giving —
that we receive. It is in pardoning — that we are
pardoned. It is in dying — that we are raised to
eternal life

— **Francis of Assisi**

Final Thought:

If I have a faith that can move mountains, but do
not have love, I am nothing!

— **1 Corinthians 13:2b**

Perseverance

James, a servant of God and of the Lord Jesus Christ, to the twelve tribes scattered among the nations: Greetings. Consider it pure joy, my brothers and sisters, whenever you face trials of many kinds, because you know that the testing of your faith produces perseverance. Let perseverance finish its work so that you may be mature and complete, not lacking anything. If any of you lacks wisdom, you should ask God, who gives generously to all without finding fault, and it will be given to you. But when you ask, you must believe and not doubt, because the one who doubts is like a wave of the sea, blown and tossed by the wind. Those who doubt should not think they will receive anything from the Lord; they are double-minded and unstable in all they do.

— James 1:1–8, 12

IN SOME CHURCHES, YOU MAY find displayed on a wall in the foyer, library or lounge a row of pictures of pastors who have served the congregation throughout its history. These portraits serve as reminders to both long-time members and newcomers of the faithfulness of the pastoral leadership of the church.

In Duluth, Minnesota, a church hung a second set of pictures on an adjoining wall. This collection displayed people the church had sent out around the world to serve as missionaries. The caption under the pastors' pictures reads: "Those Who Came to Serve." Under the pictures of those the church had commissioned as missionaries is: "Those Who Left to Serve."

A church with an effective ministry will have a great history of those who have responded to the call to come, as well as those who have responded to the call to go. Some individuals may serve for many years; others for a briefer period. Whether serving for a short season or a long time, these individuals deserve honor.

But another group of people should also be recognized. Normally, they receive little honor or commendation, yet their contribution is just as important as the other two groups. These are the volunteers who have served God in a ministry for many years. They could be described as: "Those Who Have Stayed to Serve."

In spite of increasing mobility in our society, sufficient continuity and stability is essential for effective congregational ministry. Pastors leave for another call. Young people move to college and beyond. People relocate because of changes in employment or family situations. And others leave during periods of change or difficulty.

Fortunately, however, many leaders serve faithfully for decades. And many of these people have served faithfully *behind the scenes* with little visibility and no recognition.

Perseverance is not necessarily synonymous with longevity, but it does describe well those who have finished the task that they have undertaken. In the Bible passage above, James reminds us that testing develops perseverance. This James, likely the brother of Jesus, would have observed the perseverance of Christ. Jesus' movement toward the cross was tenacious. Neither pressure from the crowds nor resistance from the Apostles deterred the Lamb of God from his reconciliatory mission.

Interestingly, James encourages us to count it all joy when we encounter trials. We read that it was for the joy set before Him that Christ endured the cross (Hebrews 12:2). A similar inner contentment and confidence becomes ours as we finish the work that God has set before us.

As members of a ministry team, you may never find your picture displayed in a prominent hallway. But those who joyfully persevere will one day hear the words of the Lord, "Well done, good and faithful servant." So continue to walk steadfastly through all the triumphs and trials that come with the call of ministry. For on a day when you feel like resigning, the Lord may be asking you to *re-sign*.

Group Exercise:

Describe one ministry area or personal area where perseverance on your part is needed. Take a moment to pray for one another.

Team Prayer:

Eternal God, We acknowledge that our view of life and ministry is often short sighted. Help us to realize that just as You control the events of history, You also control our deliberations today. Give us the perseverance to finish the task that You have assigned. Amen!

Final Thought:

When the going gets tough, the tough stay put!

Planning

To human beings belong the plans of the heart, but from the LORD comes the proper answer of the tongue. People may think all their ways are pure, but motives are weighed by the LORD. Commit to the LORD whatever you do, and he will establish your plans. The LORD works out everything to its proper end— even the wicked for a day of disaster. The LORD detests all the proud of heart. Be sure of this: They will not go unpunished. Through love and faithfulness sin is atoned for; through the fear of the LORD evil is avoided. When the LORD takes pleasure in anyone's way, he causes their enemies to make peace with them. Better a little with righteousness than much gain with injustice. In their hearts human beings plan their course, but the LORD establishes their steps.

— Proverbs 16:1–9

A SALES PERSON WAS DRIVING down a country road trying to avoid the inevitable pressures of her job. She had no specific schedule and no appointments for the day. Her attention was drawn to the side of a barn. Dozens of targets were painted in large concentric circles on the building. Inside each target was an arrow imbedded in the center of the bull's eye.

Surmising that someone who lived on the farm was an excellent marksman, she stopped to inquire about the individual's prowess. A man responded to her knock and asked, "May I help you?" "Yes," she replied. "I was driving by your farm and noticed the targets on the barn with arrows in the center of all of them. Someone must be a tremendous marksman!" "That's really no accomplishment," the man replied. "My son likes to shoot arrows into the side of the barn. Then he draws targets around them."

How many meetings have you attended over the years where the approach of no purpose, no plan and no agenda was used? How many events have you attended where things went wrong, or the outcome wasn't accomplished, because of poor planning? Teams lose missional clarity and just end up running programs when the envisioned end result isn't clear. It's been said that if you don't have any destination in mind, any road will take you there.

In Proverbs 16:1–9 the writer reminds us of the importance of planning. In meetings, for example, much time can be wasted when there is not an agenda. In classrooms, mismanagement of the clock can squeeze out time for application. And in team building, relational development (a great thing) can displace time needed for skill building (equally critical to a team's task).

Every ministry team needs to set aside time for planning. However, the amount of time required for deliberation will vary depending on the tasks to be accomplished. Scheduling different types of planning meetings, therefore, is a beneficial practice.

An annual State of the Program Meeting helps teams evaluate past performance and give direction to next year's initiatives. For a staff or church board this will look like an overall state of the church assessment. For ministry teams, such as student ministries, this will encompass an evaluation of the wellness and direction of their particular program.

Many teams have seen value in using a SWOT analysis during these annual planning events. Acquiring data on **S**trengths and **W**eaknesses (internal variables) and **O**pportunities and **T**hreats (external variables) provides valuable input. Reviewing biblical purposes and one's ministry context facilitates the setting of focused initiatives for the next year.

Periodic Strategic Planning Meetings (perhaps quarterly) are also beneficial to teams. At these meetings the progress of initiatives are evaluated, and decisions are made regarding program modifications and new initiatives.

Regular Team Meetings (usually weekly or monthly) are useful for: 1. Building camaraderie through informal sharing and the celebration of accomplishments or milestones; 2. Tactical discussions to cover the details for upcoming events; and 3. Prayer for specific people and programs.

As a ministry team, exercise discipline, direction, discernment and prayer in your planning process. But also take comfort in knowing that as you make decisions and set ministry directions, God is also at work in you and in circumstances determining your steps.

Group Exercise:

Discuss the difference between strategic and operational agenda items. Do your operational (tactical) items tend to crowd out discussion of strategic (major directional) items? Might scheduling different types of meetings assist your planning?

Team Prayer:

Sovereign God, we bring before You our agenda for today's meeting. We have some difficult decisions to make. Keep us on track. Help us to be conscious of Your sovereign control of this meeting. We commit our thoughts, our motives and our agenda to You. Amen!

A Final Thought:

Pray as though everything depends on God. Work as though everything depends on you.

— Augustine

Prejudice

My brothers and sisters, believers in our glorious
Lord Jesus Christ must not show favoritism.
Suppose someone comes into your meeting
wearing a gold ring and fine clothes, and a
poor person in filthy old clothes also comes in.
If you show special attention to the one wearing
fine clothes and say, 'Here's a good seat for you,'
but say to the one who is poor, 'You stand there'
or 'Sit on the floor by my feet,' have you not
discriminated among yourselves and become
judges with evil thoughts? Listen, my dear
brothers and sisters: Has not God chosen those
who are poor in the eyes of the world to be rich in
faith and to inherit the kingdom he promised
those who love him? But you have dishonored the
poor. Is it not the rich who are exploiting you?
Are they not the ones who are dragging you into
court? Are they not the ones who are blaspheming
the noble name of him to whom you belong? If
you really keep the royal law found in Scripture,

'Love your neighbor as yourself,' you are doing right. But if you show favoritism, you sin and are convicted by the law as lawbreakers. For whoever keeps the whole law and yet stumbles at just one point is guilty of breaking all of it. For he who said, 'You shall not commit adultery,' also said, 'You shall not murder.' If you do not commit adultery but do commit murder, you have become a lawbreaker. Speak and act as those who are going to be judged by the law that gives freedom.

— James 2:1–12

ACCORDING TO ONE DEFINITION, PREJUDICE is "a feeling, favorable or unfavorable, toward a person or thing prior to or not based on actual experience." It is simply pre-judging, or as someone described it, "Prejudice is being down on what you are not up on."

There are many kinds of prejudice (e.g., ageism, sexism, ableism), but perhaps the most prevalent is colorism. In his book, *The Nature of Prejudice*, Gordon Allport says that biases may be pro as well as con, but ethnic prejudice is mostly negative. We teach our children in Sunday school that "Jesus loves the little children, all the children of the world: Brown, red, yellow, black and white, they are precious in his sight." But for those not part of the ethnic majority of a congregation, the reality and pain of discrimination can even creep into the church.

Preference based on color can surface in subtle ways. In Spurgeon's, *The Wordless Book*, for example, children see sin as black and purity as white. Look in a dictionary some time and notice the many negative terms associated with black, and the number of positive expressions associated with white. As leaders we need to eliminate prejudice regarding people with physical features not prominent in one's majority culture.

Prejudice is not new to our generation. Christians in the early church were susceptible to the entitlement mentality of the majority culture, and discriminated against minority peoples. For example, the Jerusalem Church had to deal with prejudice against the Hellenistic widows by the Hebraic widows regarding the distribution of food (see Acts 6:1–7). Peter also learned the importance of inclusion, particularly regarding the Gentiles, through a vision that God sent him (see Acts 10).

In the scripture text above, these words from the brother of Christ were distributed to the scattered Church as a lesson for all believers, irrespective of their particular cultures. Favoritism toward the more affluent, the more popular or the more gifted is a violation of believers' oneness in Christ. In fact, any kind of discriminatory favoritism is so unlike Christ that it is considered as sinful as other lawbreaking.

Regarding racism, Pastor E. V. Hill says that one of the tasks of leaders is to "make all the *isms, wasisms*." How will this happen? It needs to begin in the hearts and minds of leaders. Leaders can provide experiences and events that will help people change their prejudice and eliminate racism. For example, we can denounce racial humor and stereotyping (either publicly or privately) as unacceptable. We can model inclusion over exclusion, and embrace our oneness in Christ over our differences in situations.

The synergy of the Body of Christ with different members all functioning together (1 Corinthians 12:12–31) makes for powerful ministry. When those we serve see very different people caring for one another, this demonstrates the reality of Christ. As leaders, let's make it happen!

Group Exercise:

Describe the dominant culture of your ministry in terms of affluence, age, race and gender. In what ways can you make your environment more welcoming of those not in the majority?

Team Prayer:

God, our Creator, help us recognize that whatever our racial and ethnic differences, we all have the same Heavenly Father. Help us celebrate diversity and not make distinctions based upon characteristics that can't be changed. We sincerely want to love our neighbors as You have loved us. Amen!

Final Thought:

God has no favorites, but He does have intimates.

— Vance Havner

Flexibility

About noon the following day as they were on
their journey and approaching the city, Peter
went up on the roof to pray. He became hungry
and wanted something to eat, and while the meal
was being prepared, he fell into a trance. He saw
heaven opened and something like a large sheet
being let down to earth by its four corners. It
contained all kinds of four-footed animals, as
well as reptiles and birds. Then a voice told him,
'Get up, Peter. Kill and eat.' 'Surely not, Lord!'
Peter replied. 'I have never eaten anything impure
or unclean.' The voice spoke to him a second
time, 'Do not call anything impure that God has
made clean.' . . . Then Peter began to speak: 'I
now realize how true it is that God does not show
favoritism but accepts those from every nation
who fear him and do what is right.'

—Acts 10: 9–15, 34–35

THIS PARTICULAR PASSAGE PROVIDES A great case study on the importance of mental and emotional flexibility. To understand its background, remember that the earliest Christians were all Jewish. Thinking that the Messiah could also be Savior for non-Jews wasn't on their radar. But it was on God's radar! The passage above is the story of a Gentile man named Cornelius who had a desire to know God, and a man named Peter who was about to have his vision of membership in God's family greatly expanded.

Needless to say, that adjustment for Peter was rather difficult. God's vision to him was repeated three times for emphasis (vv. 14–16), yet Peter still didn't understand until he went to Caesarea and met with Cornelius. After years of trying to explain to the Jews that Jesus was indeed the Messiah, now he would need to go back to the Hebraic community to convince them that Gentiles were also included in Christ's Kingdom.

The flexibility that most ministry teams need today may not be as radical as the paradigm shift required of Peter. Nevertheless, effective ministry always requires sensitivity to the Spirit's direction in our service. For example, adjustments may need to be made regarding time, day or location of meetings or changes in events. Or we may need to flex over curriculum or the amount of resources available to our specific ministry.

Flexibility is increasingly important when working with volunteers. Some of our people are young; some are retired. Some are single; some married. Some work two jobs; some are unemployed. Some have predictable schedules; others have changing schedules like shift workers or non-custodial parents.

Therefore, terms of service may need to vary within ministries, and similarly, training events may need to be scheduled at multiple times if we want 100% participation.

But perhaps the area in which we need to develop flexibility the most is in embracing team consensus over pushing our personal preferences. There's a pull within each of us that resonates with the songwriter who boasts, "I did it my way." Adam and Eve did it "my way." Pharaoh did it "my way." The Israelites in the wilderness did it "my way." Nebuchadnezzar did it "my way." And all paid the price for it!

History is replete with the disasters of doing it "my way." For, "there is a way that appears to be right, but in the end it leads to death" (Proverbs 14:12). However, note the safe contrast in the following words: "Plans fail for lack of counsel, but with many advisors they succeed" (Proverbs 15:22).

Personal trainers assert that physical well-being requires continual attention to muscle strength, aerobic capacity and structural flexibility. The importance of building service capacity is obvious to leaders. But flexibility is equally important in Christian ministry. Therefore, the continual stretching of ourselves is also essential for missional effectiveness over the long haul.

Group Exercise:

Identify some ministry areas in which your team may need more flexibility.

Team Prayer:

Father, thank You again for drawing us to Yourself through Christ, and for the opportunity to serve on this ministry team. We know that we have different backgrounds, personalities, and preferences, yet You've drawn us into a common mission. So help us to listen to Your Spirit and to one another. Grant each of us the flexibility of mind to be welcoming of ministry possibilities that You may have for us. Amen!

Final Thought:

The bow withstands enormous pressure because it is flexible!

Time

Lord, you have been our dwelling place
throughout all generations. Before the mountains
were born or you brought forth the whole world,
from everlasting to everlasting you are God. You
turn people back to dust, saying, 'Return to dust,
you mortals.' A thousand years in your sight are
like a day that has just gone by, or like a watch
in the night. Yet you sweep people away in the
sleep of death— they are like the new grass of
the morning: In the morning it springs up new,
but by evening it is dry and withered. We are
consumed by your anger and terrified by your
indignation. You have set our iniquities before
you, our secret sins in the light of your presence.
All our days pass away under your wrath; we
finish our years with a moan. Our days may
come to seventy years, or eighty, if our strength
endures; yet the best of them are but trouble and
sorrow, for they quickly pass, and we fly away.
If only we knew the power of your anger! Your

wrath is as great as the fear that is your due.
Teach us to number our days, that we may gain a
heart of wisdom.
— Psalm 90:1–12

WHILE VISITING IN THE PHILIPPINES, I [Fred] was amazed at the amount of activity at the intersections as we waited for traffic lights to change. Vendors appeared from everywhere selling newspapers, flowers, fruit, cigarettes and gum. One particular kind of purchase caught my attention. Vendors were selling one stick of gum, not a pack or a box or a carton, but one stick.

My initial response was one of bewilderment. Why would anyone take the time and effort to buy only one stick of gum? Having observed this process repeatedly, I asked the missionary who was driving why would people waste their time buying a single stick of gum.

"There are two good reasons," he replied. "First, that may be all the money they have. Secondly, today is all the time they have." Life is relatively short and tenuous in that country. Because of life's uncertainties, they enjoy life's pleasures when they can.

There are two basics views of time. Our view of time in the United States is from the linear perspective. What is past is past—we won't get it back. Time marches on. Most of the rest of the world, however, sees time from a cyclical perspective. The amount of time available is not as important as what can be done with it. If one doesn't accomplish everything today, the cycle of time will continue tomorrow.

In the New Testament, two Greek words express the difference between these two perspectives. *Chronos* describes clock time or calendar time. The word *chronology* comes from this word. When a month has ended, we rip off the calendar page because the time it represents is gone.

On the other hand, the word *kairos* describes time as the moment when something significant takes place. There are *kairos* moments in our lives like the discovery of a critical insight or the renewal of a spiritual awakening. These times are transformational and become strategic in living life from that moment on.

In Psalm 90, Moses gives us a biblical perspective on time. Since our time on earth is brief, we should learn to "number our days." Many people living today believe that since our days are finite, they should fill them with pleasure. But the pursuit of pleasure is rarely satisfying, and for most it is disappointingly shallow (expressed as "striving after wind" by the writer of Ecclesiastes).

As Christ followers, knowing that our days are numbered means we aim for lives of significance. Contributing to the lives of others creates an inner joy that's deeper than the temporal happiness of happenstances. Therefore, our days are numbered best when we honor God and serve others.

As you work together at ministry in *chronos*, schedule your events with *kairos* in mind. Use your clock hours together in service to create periods of significance in the lives of others.

Group Exercise:

Share a kairos moment in your lives.

Team Prayer:

Eternal God, thank You for the wonderful gift
of time. May we not neglect it, waste it or abuse
it. We dedicate ourselves again to Your service,
and expect something of eternal significance to
happen during our time together today. Amen!

Final Thought:

God has placed in every person an eternal
heartburn, which the temporal bicarbonates of
this world cannot burp!

— Ralph Keiper's paraphrase of Ecclesiastes 3:11

Friends

I always thank my God as I remember you in my prayers, because I hear about your love for all his people and your faith in the Lord Jesus. I pray that your partnership with us in the faith may be effective in deepening your understanding of every good thing we share for the sake of Christ. Your love has given me great joy and encouragement, because you, brother, have refreshed the hearts of the Lord's people.

— Philemon 4–7

IF YOU HAVE A MOMENT, I encourage you to read not just the verses above, but all 25 verses from this New Testament postcard. Isn't it interesting that the Holy Spirit chose to include this personal letter in our Bibles? I believe He preserved it because the letter provides a great example of friendship and forgiveness.

Paul is writing to Philemon, requesting that he welcome back, with full forgiveness, a servant who had stolen and run away from him. Some time after that event, Paul apparently led the young man into a relationship with Christ. Now he sends Onesimus back to Philemon, accompanied by this letter. The reason Paul is confident that Philemon will forgive and accept Onesimus is because of their close friendship.

No doubt it's easier to connect with friends today than it was in Paul's day. Yet, requirements for relationship building have remained similar over time. From this letter we can observe that friendships are developed through *regular communication, thoughtful encouragement, generous forgiveness* and *persistent teamwork*.

Friendships are developed through regular communication (v. 1–3). In Paul's opening salutation he greets Philemon and Apphia (perhaps his wife), Archippus (a leader in the church) and the other members of that house church. The Apostle likely led Philemon and his family to Christ (v. 19), and would visit in his home on his journeys through Colossae. Though away from them because of his imprisonment, Paul maintained correspondence with them. He also hoped to visit them when he was freed from prison (v. 22).

This letter was carried by hand from Paul to Philemon. Yet today we can meet face to face, place phone calls, write emails or send text messages. So let me encourage you to go deeper with one another in your relationships as friends. Don't limit your communication to ministry details. Share your personal concerns, as Paul did in this letter. The result will be greater joy and deeper richness in your service.

Friendships are developed through thoughtful encouragement. In the passage above Paul thanks God for Philemon, and also expresses his appreciation directly to his friend. Philemon is an encourager, and Paul encouraged him to keep on "refreshing the hearts of the saints" (v. 7). Certainly there are times for correcting a friend (Proverbs 27:6), but it is in the context of encouragement and affirmation that correction is more easily received. One author has said that it takes 10 "at-a-boys" to offset each "you dummy." Being human, it's easy to see when someone drops the ball. Nevertheless, friends encourage one another to move forward positively (see Hebrews 10:24).

Friendships are developed through generous forgiveness. Beginning in verse 8, Paul expressed the main reason for writing. Paul asks Philemon to forgive Onesimus because: It's the right things to do (v. 8); its the loving things to do (v. 9); Onesimus is Paul's spiritual son (v. 10); he will now be useful (v. 11); he is Philemon's spiritual brother (v. 16); Paul and Philemon are partners in ministry (v. 17); Philemon owes Paul (v. 19); and Paul desires for Philemon to refresh his own heart (v. 20).

Wow! Paul can lay down a heavy argument. But it's not the logic of Paul's appeal that will affect the decision of Philemon. It's knowing the Christ-like heart of his dear friend that leads Paul to assume that Philemon "will do even more" than he asks (v. 21).

Members of every ministry team are human. While each is a new creation in Christ, each also has an old nature. Misunderstandings will happen; offenses will occur. Only in the soil of generous forgiveness can friendships flourish.

Friendships are developed through persistent teamwork. If you read this letter in its entirety you noticed additional people mentioned: Timothy, Epaphras, Mark, Aristarchus, Demas and Luke. In this letter Paul refers to them simply as "fellow workers." But elsewhere in the New Testament they are recognized as prayer warriors, pastors, messengers, writers and church planters. No doubt their friendships were deepened through their co-labor over time. For people who work hard toward a common purpose draw closer together in relationship.

Friendships exist on a relational continuum. At one end we have acquaintanceships; at the other end we have soul mates. In a typical ministry team, relationships will vary along the continuum. No doubt Paul was closer to Timothy and Luke than to Philemon and Archippus. Our passions and personalities will mean we connect more deeply with some people than with others. Nevertheless, the more closely you work together as friends (rather than mere coworkers), the greater will be your impact on those you serve.

Group Exercise:

In a circle response, have the members of your team share a word of encouragement to the person seated on their right.

Team Prayer:

Father, thanks for not only drawing us into a relationship with You, but also into the family of Christ. Deepen our friendships with one another as brothers and sisters in the Lord. May we be slow to criticize, but quick to encourage. May we take the initiative in communicating. May we be generous in forgiveness. And may we serve diligently together as an offering to You. Amen!

Final Thought:

By this will everyone know that you're My
disciples: if you love one another.

— John 13:35

Complaining

Now the people complained about their hardships in the hearing of the LORD, and when he heard them his anger was aroused. Then fire from the LORD burned among them and consumed some of the outskirts of the camp. When the people cried out to Moses, he prayed to the LORD and the fire died down. So that place was called Taberah, because fire from the LORD had burned among them. The rabble with them began to crave other food, and again the Israelites started wailing and said, 'If only we had meat to eat! We remember the fish we ate in Egypt at no cost— also the cucumbers, melons, leeks, onions and garlic. But now we have lost our appetite; we never see anything but this manna!' . . . Moses heard the people of every family wailing at the entrance to their tents. The LORD became exceedingly angry, and Moses was troubled. He asked the LORD, 'Why have you brought this trouble on your servant? What have I done to displease you

that you put the burden of all these people on me?
Did I conceive all these people? Did I give them
birth? Why do you tell me to carry them in my
arms, as a nurse carries an infant, to the land
You promised on oath to their ancestors? Where
can I get meat for all these people? They keep
wailing to me, 'Give us meat to eat!' I cannot
carry all these people by myself; the burden is too
heavy for me. If this is how you are going to treat
me, please go ahead and kill me— if I have found
favor in your eyes— and do not let me face my
own ruin.'

— Numbers 11:1–6, 10–15

THE BIBLE ADMONISHES EVERYTHING THAT has breath to "Praise the Lord" (Psalm 150:6). It also warns us to "let no unwholesome speech come from our mouths" (Ephesians 4:29). And the New Testament letters continually remind us to "encourage one another," "build up one another," "do good to one another" and "lovingly bear with one another."

So why is it that, even in our faith communities, we hear so much complaining? Perhaps it's because we live in an entitlement culture, or because we have too high of an opinion of ourselves, thinking we deserve more than we do.

A propensity toward complaining is not new to our times. In the Old Testament we observe that the Israelites were highly skilled at this negative practice. And in the biblical narrative above, God made it pretty clear how He felt about their critical spirit.

In this account, the people first complained about their so-called hardships. So quickly they had forgotten their oppression in Egypt. In response to their criticism, God sent a judgment of fire to burn the perimeter of the camp. God gave them a visual demonstration of His displeasure with their murmuring (1–3).

Ignoring this warning, they complained again, this time about their limited diet. In response, God judged them with a plague, slaying the instigators ("the rabble among them" see 4–9 and 31–34). In essence, the people were saying: God, we know better than You do how we should live and what we should eat. And God judged their unbelief and disobedience.

A third complaint was spoken by Moses, who really unloaded on God (see 11–15). Rather strong words, right? But instead of judging Moses for his griping, God responded positively toward him. God gave Moses:

1. Assistance. "I will take some of the power of the Spirit that is on you and put it on them [70 leaders] so that you will not have to carry it [the burden of ministry] alone" (vv. 16, 17); and

2. Counsel. "Tell the people . . ." (v. 18). God advises him on how to handle the people.

Now, anyone reading this passage would likely question: Why did God judge the Israelites, yet provide an affirming response to Moses? A careful analysis would suggest two reasons.

First, the people had self-centered, unjust complaints, whereas Moses had a legitimate complaint—he could not handle the load. But more significantly, the people talked to each other about their concerns, slandering the Lord and His chosen leader. Moses, on the other hand, took his concern directly to God.

God designed us to be people of praise. So as leaders let's put off any negative speech about particular people or situations. Instead, let's first talk to God about our concerns, then when necessary and with His counsel, address the person(s) involved. Never are we free to criticize a brother or sister to another party. Slander is unbecoming of Christ's shepherds. Instead, "let us only speak what is helpful for building up others" (Ephesians 4:29).

Group Exercise:

Take a few moments for silent prayer. Individually, privately, pour out your greatest complaint to God. Then in pairs, without sharing the specific concerns, ask God for His peace and His leading in each other's situation.

Team Prayer:

Father, we agree with the Apostle James that the tongue is a fire that can destroy. Instead of being a grouchy, complaining people, help us remain positive. Keep us from slandering one another, especially those whom You've placed in leadership. May our voices be instruments of praise to You and encouragement to one another. Amen!

Final Thought:

Words from the mouth reveal attitudes in the heart.

Diplomacy

'So then, tell me the dream, and I will know that you can interpret it for me.' The astrologers answered the king, 'There is not a person on earth who can do what the king asks! No king, however great and mighty, has ever asked such a thing of any magician or enchanter or astrologer. What the king asks is too difficult. No one can reveal it to the king except the gods, and they do not live among human beings.' This made the king so angry and furious that he ordered the execution of all the wise men of Babylon. So the decree was issued to put the wise men to death, and men were sent to look for Daniel and his friends to put them to death. When Arioch, the commander of the king's guard, had gone out to put to death the wise men of Babylon, Daniel spoke to him with wisdom and tact. He asked the king's officer, 'Why did the king issue such a harsh decree?' Arioch then explained the matter to Daniel. At this, Daniel went in to the king and

asked for time, so that he might interpret the
dream for him.
— Daniel 2:9b–16

HOWARD COSELL WAS ONE OF the best-known sportscasters in America. Some people thought he was great, while others disliked him. You never had to wonder what Cosell meant. When someone questioned the manner he used to express himself, he would often respond, "I'm just telling it like it is." Few people questioned Cosell's knowledge of the game or the accuracy of his comments. Many, however, challenged his lack of tact. In fact, it was because of this impropriety that the sports network eventually let him go.

Some people believe that telling it like it is (no matter whom it hurts) is a virtue. But as Christians we understand that truth speaking requires love as its companion (Ephesians 4:15). Furthermore, the scriptures admonish us to be patient and forgiving in spirit. For some, telling it like it is vents their frustration. But a godly response requires more. A Christian leader's focus must be on the nurture of others. Therefore even confrontation must be delivered with love.

Biblical diplomacy requires both *wisdom* and *tact.* Daniel, a wonderful example, demonstrated a skillful use of these two qualities. Even before serving as a diplomat under King Nebuchadnezzar, he displayed the quality of diplomacy.

While living in captivity in Babylon, Daniel and his three friends acquired a broad range of knowledge in many areas of life. He was considered one of the wisest men in his alien country. When a group of wise men were unable to interpret the king's nightmare, Nebuchadnezzar condemned all the country's wise men to death. Even though Daniel was not part of the group who was unable to interpret the king's dream, he was included in the death warrant.

When Daniel heard the decree from Arioch, the commander of the king's guard, "Daniel spoke to him with wisdom and tact" (v. 14). Wisdom is not simply the accumulation of knowledge. It also includes the ability to use sound judgment and discernment. Tact is the ability to say and do the right thing, at the right time, in the right way. It has been described as the ability to make a point without making an enemy.

Diplomacy for a Christian leader may occasionally call for telling it like it is, but *how* we convey the message may be more important than the message itself. Our personal demeanor greatly influences the recipient's acceptance of a message. Daniel displayed his wisdom and tact by asking questions of Arioch, and then listening to his reply (v. 15). He further displayed wisdom by asking the king for more time. Daniel needed to find his three friends in order to spend time in discussion and prayer.

The context of your service today as a ministry team is quite different than that of Daniel's day. But while circumstances change, relational work among people remains relatively similar. So build up one another and those you serve. Avoid rushing to judgments. Never use humor at another's expense. Guard against sarcasm and cynicism. As you work together as a team, let your gracious speech and relational tact help you accomplish your mission.

Group Exercise:

Confidentially discuss a specific situation or individual where tactful admonishment is warranted. Decide who will approach the person. Pray for a God-honoring outcome.

Team Prayer:

LORD, thank You for the privilege of being Your children and serving as leaders. May we always tell the truth. And especially help us communicate truth with wisdom, tact and love. May we constantly be aware that we are Your representatives. Amen!

Final Thought:

A spoonful of sugar helps the medicine go down.

— Mary Poppins

Problems

They came back to Moses and Aaron and the whole Israelite community at Kadesh in the Desert of Paran. There they reported to them and to the whole assembly and showed them the fruit of the land. They gave Moses this account: 'We went into the land to which you sent us, and it does flow with milk and honey! Here is its fruit. But the people who live there are powerful, and the cities are fortified and very large. We even saw descendants of Anak there. The Amalekites live in the Negev; the Hittites, Jebusites and Amorites live in the hill country; and the Canaanites live near the sea and along the Jordan.' Caleb silenced the people before Moses and said, 'We should go up and take possession of the land, for we can certainly do it.' But the men who had gone up with him said, 'We can't attack those people; they are stronger than we are.' And they spread among the Israelites a bad report about the land they had explored. They said, 'The land

> we explored devours those living in it. All the
> people we saw there are of great size. We saw the
> Nephilim there (the descendants of Anak come
> from the Nephilim). We seemed like grasshoppers
> in our own eyes, and we looked the same to them.'
>
> — Numbers 13:26–33

EVERYONE FACES PROBLEMS AND OBSTACLES. Some people try to ignore them. Others try to push them on someone else. Problems can be ignored, transferred to someone else or faced, but few problems go away by themselves. In the devotional passage above, Israel is facing a literally big problem—giants!

God told Moses to send a representative from each tribe to explore the land of Canaan. The purpose of their recognizance was not to see if it was possible to take the land, for God had already promised it to them (Numbers 13:2). Their explanation was simply to authenticate God's appraisal that the land was indeed flowing with milk and honey.

Notice that all of the spies saw the same things; all recorded the same data. "We went into the land to which you sent us and it does flow with milk and honey! Here is its fruit." But they also added, "but the people who live there are powerful, and the cities are fortified and very large" (vv. 27, 28).

The difference among the spies was not in the data, but in the interpretation of the data. Ten spies brought back a negative report. "The land we explored devours those living in it. All the people we saw there were of great size" (v. 32). However, two other spies, Caleb and Joshua, drew a different conclusion: "We should go up and take possession of the land, for we can certainly do it" (v. 30).

The difference between the two reports came down to a difference in perspective. Both groups agreed that there were giants in the land, but for one group the giants were bigger than their God, while for the other group God was much bigger than their giants. The majority report highlighted their finite limitations: "We seem like grasshoppers in our eyes, and we look the same to them" (v.33). Whereas Joshua and Caleb highlighted the greatness of God: "If the Lord is pleased with us, He will lead us into that land . . . do not be afraid of the people of the land, because we will swallow them up. Their protection is gone, but the Lord is with us. Do not be afraid of them" (14:8, 9).

Leaders don't need to be in ministry long before they run into problems. According to Murphy's Law, "Whatever can go wrong, will go wrong." One of our colleagues has his own Erickson's law which holds: "Murphy was an optimist!" Problems are a reality of life.

So when your team encounters problems, resistance, barriers or attacks, remember the size of the One who called you into this mission. He is all knowing, all powerful and the Lord of all circumstances. Problems are placed in perspective when we view them next to our Sovereign God.

Group Exercise:

Identify a problem or challenge that is (or potentially might be) affecting your ministry. How might God have you deal with this problem?

Team Prayer:

Almighty God, we lay before You all of the problems and obstacles that we have encountered and may encounter in the future. Some of them are rather insignificant and others overwhelm us. Help us to bring them all to You. We are confident that You will guide us and lead us into all righteousness and truth. Amen!

Final Thought:

You must live with people to know their problems, and live with God in order to solve them.

— **Peter T. Forsyth**

Resistance to Change

Though I am free and belong to no one, I have made myself a slave to everyone, to win as many as possible. To the Jews I became like a Jew, to win the Jews. To those under the law I became like one under the law (though I myself am not under the law), so as to win those under the law. To those not having the law I became like one not having the law (though I am not free from God's law but am under Christ's law), so as to win those not having the law. To the weak I became weak, to win the weak. I have become all things to all people so that by all possible means I might save some. I do all this for the sake of the gospel, that I may share in its blessings.

— 1 Corinthians 9:19–23

EACH OF US COULD SHARE war stories about people's resistance to change. Sometimes the resistance is mild. Other times it comes in the form of blackmail (e.g., "If you change our program, we'll quit coming"). Variety may be the spice of life, but people are also creatures of habit. They resist things that cause them discomfort.

Resistance to change is not unique to the ministry. However, the nature of our task makes managing change especially difficult. First, we have an unchanging message, and implementing change may appear like we are tinkering with the message. Second, we work with volunteers, and therefore we do not have the clout that government, business or other institutions may have to implement change. Third, our communities are considered a family, and we do not want to offend anyone, especially the proverbial weaker brother.

But we know in our hearts and from experience that resistance to change can paralyze an organization. Therefore, a ministry desirous of spiritual transformation must use all possible means to point people to Christ and present them mature in Him. While biblical purposes remain unmovable, the means of accomplishing these purposes must remain flexible. To state it in familiar terms, our commitment is to *function* rather than *form*.

Notice in the devotional passage above how innovative Paul was in his approach to ministry. He was eager to try new things—anything that would help people discover Jesus and accept Him as Lord. He frequently encountered resistance, yet pushed forward strategically in presenting Christ.

Likewise, leaders today need to move forward with changes that will strengthen ministry effectiveness. By following four proven practices your team can encourage receptivity to change.

Create an atmosphere where change is acceptable. Individual programs are merely vehicles of ministry. They are formats for accomplishing biblical purposes. When a change is needed, we can foster some healthy discontent to help people see the limitations of an existing format. Then by regularly painting a vision of possibilities, we can establish a culture where dreaming is encouraged, and necessary changes are accepted.

Build trust in leadership. People are more willing to follow leaders with demonstrated integrity. Therefore, as a leadership team establish a track record of credibility. Keep commitments, fulfill your promises, be available and communicate your motives. These practices will help people understand why a specific change will be beneficial.

Make sure a specific change is the best alternative. Seek input from those who will be affected by the anticipated change. Early in the process win the support of the influencers among those you serve. With good input in hand, a small change group can then utilize problem-solving techniques to select the best solution.

Communicate change early and thoroughly. Conveying ideas in familiar terms is an essential part of the change process. And personally communicating with people the rationale and implementation strategy will go a long way. Some leaders err by trying to squelch opposition, but allowing for disagreement is a better long term strategy for assuring acceptance. By anticipating resistance, depersonalizing dissent, yet affirming the value of an innovation, most people will get on board with a new initiative.

Almost everyone believes that change is important. We would rather drive our cars to work than walk. We would rather catch the news on the Internet than wait for a messenger to herald word by foot. We would rather use indoor plumbing than an outhouse. Change is not bad; rather it is helpful. Nevertheless, occasionally you will hear the cry: "Is this change really necessary?"

If those you are serving have confidence in you and understand the reasons behind a change, they will likely offer less resistance to new forms that will enable them to better carry out their biblical mandate.

Group Exercise:

Identify a specific change that could benefit your ministry. Brainstorm a few potential action items for each of the four steps of the change process.

Team Prayer:

Heavenly Father, we are thankful that You are a God who doesn't change. Give us the willingness to change our approach to best be in synch with Your redemptive program. Then give us discipline, sensitivity, discernment and determination as we take the necessary steps to bring the new future into reality. Amen!

Final Thought:

The only human institution which rejects
progress is the cemetery.
— Harold Wilson

Tolerance

To the angel of the church in Thyatira write:
These are the words of the Son of God, whose
eyes are like blazing fire and whose feet are like
burnished bronze. I know your deeds, your love
and faith, your service and perseverance, and
that you are now doing more than you did at
first. Nevertheless, I have this against you: You
tolerate that woman Jezebel, who calls herself
a prophet. By her teaching she misleads my
servants into sexual immorality and the eating
of food sacrificed to idols. I have given her time
to repent of her immorality, but she is unwilling.
So I will cast her on a bed of suffering, and I will
make those who commit adultery with her suffer
intensely, unless they repent of her ways. I will
strike her children dead. Then all the churches
will know that I am he who searches hearts and
minds, and I will repay each of you according
to your deeds. Now I say to the rest of you in
Thyatira, to you who do not hold to her teaching

> and have not learned Satan's so-called deep
> secrets, 'I will not impose any other burden on
> you, except to hold on to what you have until I
> come.' To those who are victorious and do my will
> to the end, I will give authority over the nations—
> they 'will rule them with an iron scepter and will
> dash them to pieces like pottery'— just as I have
> received authority from my Father. I will also
> give them the morning star. Whoever has ears, let
> them hear what the Spirit says to the churches.
>
> — Revelation 2:18–29

THE CHURCH HAS SOMETIMES BEEN pictured as a boat. As the church sails along life's journey, it needs to make sure the boat is in the water, rather than the water in the boat.

One surge of water that often pushes at the boat is *hedonism* the love of pleasure. This threat is not new to our generation. In fact, it was a specific problem that Jesus confronted and condemned in the church in Thyatira. Water had gotten into the boat and no one wanted to do anything about it.

A leading woman in the church, referred to as Jezebel, was teaching that it was all right for people to eat food sacrificed to idols and to participate in sexual immorality. Those like her who teach or practice immorality are assured of judgment. But notice that Jesus also condemns those who are aware of such practices and tolerate them.

Toleration is actually a neutral word, as are words like moderation and persuasion. Whether they are good or bad depends upon the object.

To be a tolerant person in our society is viewed as a positive trait. It means to be *understanding, unprejudiced, fair, broadminded and charitable.* We are encouraged by the media to be tolerant of other people's beliefs and behavior. However, this generally positive practice can become negatively harmful when the church becomes tolerant of heretical teaching and immoral behavior in its midst. In this latter case tolerance can also mean that *we have become lenient, permissive, soft, easy and indulgent.*

Many Christians are reticent to interfere with another believer's lifestyle choices. "It's not my business. What people do and how they live is a private matter." These statements reflect a prevalent attitude in many religious circles. But while beliefs and behavior in the church may be personal, in reality they can never be private. Personal sin always affects others.

Ever since the days of the church at Thyatira, Christian organizations have been devastated because leaders have tolerated water in the boat. It's never the wrong time to fix the leaks! So as leaders, while avoiding prideful judgmentalness, intervene when necessary to help those embracing destructive behaviors.

Group Exercise:

Identify several areas where the cultural value of tolerance tries to thwart biblical values. How does a Christ follower best interact with an increasingly post-Christian culture?

Team Prayer:

Holy God, We want to be pure and clean in Your sight both as individuals and as a team. May this ministry be a place where people are accepted and loved whatever their past. At the same time, help us to love fellow Christians enough to confront them when they blatantly disregard Your Word. Lord, this will be hard. So when necessary, help us not to come across with a judgmental attitude, but rather with an attitude of warmth and concern. Amen!

Final Thought:

We are too Christian really to enjoy sinning and too fond of sinning really to enjoy Christianity. Most of us know perfectly well what we ought to do: our trouble is that we don't want to do it.

— Peter Marshall

Listening

The next day Moses took his seat to serve as judge
for the people, and they stood around him from
morning till evening. When his father-in-law
saw all that Moses was doing for the people, he
said, 'What is this you are doing for the people?
Why do you alone sit as judge, while all these
people stand around you from morning till
evening?' Moses answered him, 'Because the
people come to me to seek God's will. Whenever
they have a dispute, it is brought to me, and I
decide between the parties and inform them of
God's decrees and instructions.' Moses' father-in-
law replied, 'What you are doing is not good. You
and these people who come to you will only wear
yourselves out. The work is too heavy for you;
you cannot handle it alone. Listen now to me
and I will give you some advice, and may God
be with you.' . . . Moses listened to his father-in-
law and did everything he said. He chose capable
men from all Israel and made them leaders of the

> people, officials over thousands, hundreds, fifties
> and tens. They served as judges for the people
> at all times. The difficult cases they brought
> to Moses, but the simple ones they decided
> themselves.

— Exodus 18:13–19a; 24–26

GOOD COMMUNICATION SKILLS ARE IMPORTANT for effective leaders. But when people hear the word *communication*, they immediately associate it with talking. Yes, good communication includes articulate, engaging speech. But too often overlooked, it also includes effective listening.

Listening is important in order to hear the quiet voice of God. Listening is important to hear the perspectives of our teammates. And listening is important to understand those we serve.

Researchers break down the communication process this way: writing (9%), reading (16%), talking (35%) and listening (40%). Good communication utilizes listening more than other related skills. Many leaders have refined speaking skills through readings, taking classes or watching presentations by good communicators. But few, when asked, report studying the art of listening.

In the Bible text above, Moses' father-in-law, Jethro, observed that Moses was exhausting himself in his counseling/mediation role with the Israelites. Jethro pulled his son-in-law aside and gave him advice on delegation (see meditation entitled *Delegation*). The text records Moses' response: "Moses *listened* to his father-in-law and did everything he said" (v. 24). Moses implemented Jethro's advice, and positive results followed for Moses personally and for the people corporately.

While the above story demonstrates the beauty of listening, we know how hard it is to really practice this skill. Each of us has filters of interests, beliefs, feelings, assumptions, prejudices, expectations and experiences that influence what we hear. In addition, sometimes we're turned off by the perceived attitudes or demeanor of the person speaking.

In the book of Proverbs we see a number of comparisons and contrasts. One repeated contrast is between the wise person and the fool. Regarding listening, this book of wisdom warns: "He who answers before listening—that is his folly and his shame" (18:13). By way of contrast it also invites: "A wise person listens to advice" (12:15b).

As leaders and role models, avoid practices that hinder communication such as:

◆ Not making eye contact

◆ Looking at your watch, materials or other people

◆ Multitasking (such as shuffling papers)

Instead, look for ways to:

◆ Focus on another's message not the speaker's mannerisms

◆ Listen holistically including words, tone and body language

◆ Ask questions for clarification and additional details

◆ Summarize mentally, and out loud when appropriate

The more effective our listening skills, the better will be our teamwork, and the more transformational will be our ministry.

Group Exercise:

At the conclusion of your meeting, refer back to the listening practices above.

How well did you do in attending to one another?

Team Prayer:

Father, help us to become better listeners— to those You have called us to serve, to one another and especially to You. Sometimes out of enthusiasm, and sometimes out of strong opinions, we interrupt and push our particular viewpoints. In humility, remind us that You speak to many, not just to one. May we not be like the foolish, but the wise, who are quick to listen. Amen!

Final Thought:

. . . everyone should be quick to listen, slow to speak and slow to become angry. . . .

— James 1:19

Servanthood

When he had finished washing their feet, he put
on his clothes and returned to his place. 'Do you
understand what I have done for you?'
He asked them. 'You call me 'Teacher' and
'Lord,' and rightly so, for that is what I am. Now
that I, your Lord and Teacher, have washed your
feet, you also should wash one another's feet. I
have set you an example that you should do as
I have done for you. Very truly I tell you,
servants are not greater than their master, nor
are messengers greater than the one who sent
them. Now that you know these things, you
will be blessed if you do them.'

— John 13:12–17

THE CONTEXT OF THIS PASSAGE is the Passover meal—the
Last Supper that Jesus shared with His disciples. Earlier in the
evening the 12 engaged in yet another argument over which of
them would be greatest in the coming Kingdom. In response

to their arrogance, and to answer their question, Jesus assumed the position of a servant and began washing their feet.

Through His act of servanthood, Jesus demonstrated the countercultural values of God's Kingdom. He explained that true greatness is found in the heart of a humble servant. If the disciples wanted to follow Jesus, they would also need to embrace his principle of servanthood.

From this passage we can glean several Guidelines for Servanthood:

Make sure your hands are clean. Jesus explained the difference between cleansing and washing. Although the disciples were clean after bathing, their feet had become dirty by the end of the day. Cleansing one's heart does not need to be repeated, but washing the filth of sin from one's feet and hands needs to be repeated periodically. All of the disciples (except Judas) had pure hearts, but they needed to make sure their hands were washed before they ministered to others.

Do not get the water too hot. Washing one's feet should be soothing and relaxing. Yet this passage records Peter's resistance to Christ's service. Jesus could easily have rebuked Peter for his defiant attitude. Instead He gently restored him. We cannot minister to people when we have a harsh or critical spirit.

Do not wait for people's feet to be clean. I don't know which disciple's feet Jesus washed first. It might have been Judas', or perhaps it was Peter's. The point is, Jesus did not wait for people to have perfumed feet. It is not difficult to wash the feet of prominent or lovely people. It is harder to humble ourselves before a critic or unkind person. Yet true love goes beyond selective service.

Be willing to let other people wash your feet. Peter would have gladly washed the feet of Jesus. He was even willing to die for Jesus. However, Peter did not want Jesus to wash his feet or die for him. It may be more blessed to give than to receive, but it has been my experience that it is more difficult to receive than it is to give. When I give, I am in control. When I receive, the roles are reversed. No one can enjoy the gift of giving unless another accepts the gift of receiving.

Today, with daily showers, fresh socks, laced shoes and paved roads, most Christians don't practice foot-washing. Nevertheless, the transcultural principle of humble service, frequently demonstrated by Jesus, is a universal mandate for Christ followers.

As members of a ministry team, you will notice that opportunities for servanthood always emerge. A servant heart, for example, can be recognized when a person is willing to take minutes at meetings. Christ-like servanthood can also be seen in the person who remains to clean up or reset a room after a program. For each of us there are unlimited ways that we can join Jesus in taking up the basin and towel.

Group Exercise:

If you were to figuratively pick up the basin and towel, whose feet do you sense God would like you to wash at this present time?

Team Prayer:

Lord, it is difficult to love everyone. We find it easy to love lovely people. However, You love everyone whether they are lovely or not. Help us to be moved with compassion to minister to everyone. Amen!

Final Thought:

Does anyone who knows me well call me a servant?

— Howard Hendricks

Civility

Let everyone be subject to the governing authorities, for there is no authority except that which God has established. The authorities that exist have been established by God. Consequently, whoever rebels against the authority is rebelling against what God has instituted, and those who do so will bring judgment on themselves. For rulers hold no terror for those who do right, but for those who do wrong. Do you want to be free from fear of the one in authority? Then do what is right and you will be commended. For the one in authority is God's servant for your good. But if you do wrong, be afraid, for rulers do not bear the sword for no reason. They are God's servants, agents of wrath to bring punishment on the wrongdoer. Therefore, it is necessary to submit to the authorities, not only because of possible punishment but also as a matter of conscience.

This is also why you pay taxes, for the authorities are God's servants, who give their full time to governing. Give to everyone what you owe: If you owe taxes, pay taxes; if revenue, then revenue; if respect, then respect; if honor, then honor. Let no debt remain outstanding, except the continuing debt to love one another, for whoever loves others has fulfilled the law. The commandments, 'You shall not commit adultery,' 'You shall not murder,' 'You shall not steal,' 'You shall not covet,' and whatever other command there may be, are summed up in this one command: 'Love your neighbor as yourself.' Love does no harm to its neighbor. Therefore love is the fulfillment of the law.

— Romans 13:1–10

ONE OF THE PARADOXES OF Scripture is that Christ followers are citizens of both heaven and earth. In the words of Jesus we are to "give to Caesar what is Caesar's, and give to God what is God's" (Matthew 22:21). Our earthly civic responsibility is also addressed by Paul in the above text. He details a Christian's obligation to government and to neighbors.

In this passage he first reminds believers that submission to civic leaders naturally follows submission to God, for God "has established the governing authorities." We may protest the oppressiveness of evil governments and challenge policies that we deem immoral, but governance itself is God's plan for humanity.

The government exists to provide security (v. 3). As Christians we should be thankful for a government that deals with local threats (such as drunk drivers or violations of building codes), as well as international threats (such as warring nations and terrorism).

The government also exists to do community good (v. 4). Likewise, as citizens we are grateful for good roads, schools, DMV's, parks, patent offices, the FDA and the CDC. And we are grateful to live in a nation where people from disadvantaged children to frail seniors are a societal concern.

It follows, therefore, that Christians should support their government. And Paul explains that this happens in two ways (see v.7).

First, we submit *by paying taxes and revenue*. In Paul's day there was a ground tax, an income tax and a poll tax. These are equivalent to our federal taxes. Rome also had import taxes, road taxes and bridge taxes, customs taxes, and even vehicle taxes for wagons. These revenues are equivalent to our state or local taxes. Christians, as citizens, don't grudgingly pay taxes. We submit what is due, recognizing the good that government can do with this revenue.

Second, we submit *by paying respect and honor* to governing officials. This means recognizing the weight of their responsibilities. It also requires praying for our president, senators, representatives, governors, legislators and mayors. While political jokes and caricatures may be funny, let's not be a part of demeaning those who will one day give an account to God for their civic leadership. Rather than criticizing public figures, the Bible instructs us to support them.

As citizens of earth, awaiting full citizenship in heaven, our civic responsibility also extends to those living in our neighborhoods. In this passage, we are not only told how to treat governing authorities, but we are also guided in how to treat those living around us. God's Spirit, speaking through the apostle Paul, sums it up this way: "Love your neighbor as yourself. Love does no harm to its neighbor. Therefore, love is the fulfillment of the law" (Romans: 13:9–10).

As leaders let's not extend civility only to those we serve in our various ministries. Rather, let's also consider the neighbors in the surrounding community. Neighbors in proximity to a church, for example, put up with extra traffic and extra noise. So as Christian citizens think about what you may occasionally do for them. What good is it if we run a great program, but don't let the light of Christ's Kingdom shine in our neighborhoods?

As Christians consider the benefits we have today because of government. Always be prayerful regarding legislative and civic concerns. And make a commitment to respect governing authorities.

Group Exercise:

Brainstorm possibilities, and then select one specific way to show appreciation to the neighbors who surround your ministry.

Team Prayer:

Father, we ask that You would help us to be good citizens of Your Kingdom and of the society in which You have placed us. We want to be Your ambassadors, letting our neighbors see the salt and light of Your Kingdom. We long for the day of the new heaven and earth, with you dwelling among us. Until then, through the power of Your Spirit, may Your presence been seen through our civility. Amen!

Final Thought:

The more profoundly one is concerned about heaven, the more deeply one cares about God's will being done on earth.

— J. I. Packer

Simplicity

As Jesus and his disciples were on their way, he came to a village where a woman named Martha opened her home to him. She had a sister called Mary, who sat at the Lord's feet listening to what he said. But Martha was distracted by all the preparations that had to be made. She came to him and asked, 'Lord, don't you care that my sister has left me to do the work by myself? Tell her to help me!' 'Martha, Martha,' the Lord answered, 'you are worried and upset about many things, but few things are needed— or indeed only one. Mary has chosen what is better, and it will not be taken away from her.'

— Luke 10:38–42

AS NEWLYWEDS, MY WIFE AND I [John] headed out to seminary towing a 4x6 U-Haul containing our few worldly possessions.

Two years later we left Denver for a new ministry in Arizona. This time we transported our stuff in a small Ryder truck. Eight years after that we moved to New Jersey and needed half a United Van Lines trailer to haul all of our belongings. Six years later we moved to Minnesota filling nearly all of a 45-foot Allied Van. How is it that we collect so much baggage on our journey through life? While this might make a good subject for another meditation, for now let me suggest that the same phenomenon occurs in churches and parachurch organizations.

Christians in the early church met in homes; three centuries later they owned common property and buildings. Over the years the buildings escalated in size, as did programs and budgets. Life stage programming was embraced next, with special ministries to children, youth and adults. With growth, churches added multiple worship services, many with concurrent educational programs. Next, youth meetings were developed, followed by children's church time. Vacation Bible Schools have become a staple, and club programs have proliferated. Music ministries have flourished with different styles of worship provided even within a given congregation. Ushering has developed from a pick-up game just before the offering, to an orchestrated team effort, seating people and distributing bulletins (wherever bulletins came from). And don't forget small groups, assimilation teams, men's ministries, women's ministries, the media center, as well as dozens of ministry teams serving both the faith community and various neighborhoods.

Fifty years ago we didn't solicit people to lead the youth mission; 100 years ago we didn't burn out teachers in summer day camps; and 1,800 years ago we didn't need personnel for a decorations committee.

Now, I'm not saying we should scrap all of our programs. In fact, I advocate specialized programs for ministry growth. But the question still remains: "When is enough, enough?"

I love the above devotional passage. By its inclusion in our Bibles, the Holy Spirit believes we can all learn from the message in its narrative. On the surface it might look like Jesus is putting down Martha. But remember, it was Martha's home into which Jesus was invited. And it was through her hospitality that she demonstrated her love for Christ. Furthermore, upon the death of her brother, Lazarus, it's Martha who first went to meet Jesus with a trust that affirmed: "If you had been here, my brother would not have died" (John 11:21). And later with remarkable faith she declared: "I believe that you are the Christ, the Son of God, who was to come into the world" (v 27).

In the passage above, we see that Martha's heart was right, but her priorities at that moment were misguided. In fact the text says that she "was distracted by all the preparations that had to be made" (v. 39). Yes, there's a time for preparing dinner. In fact, there's a time for everything under the sun (Ecclesiastes 3). But everything under the sun cannot be done all at the same time. And today, many Christian ministries are coming to that same conclusion— not everything has to be done at once, and not everything has to be done by us.

The philosophy that drove the proliferation of church programming can be summarized this way: "We need to reach people where they are and meet their needs." The result was that the greater the diversity and abundance of programming, the more people could be reached. But in the wake of that approach, ministries have been left with burned-out servants, huge facility debt and a great amount of frustration.

Today, a growing number of Christian organizations are moving away from that philosophy. Rather than giving people *everything they want*, thriving ministries are focusing more on *what people need* and what their mission *can do best.*

Pastors of significant churches and researchers alike are calling for clarity of focus. This is not just because facilities, finances and volunteerism are stretched. It's predominately because of a growing recognition that missional success is more likely when greater resources are poured into fewer ministries. Let me share the observations from a few leaders to illustrate this point.

In *The Present Future*, Reggie McNeil argues for churches to develop a *score card* on what really matters to their mission. Similarly, in *The Seven Practices of Effective Churches*, Andy Stanley states that each church must define its *win*. In other words, when we have accomplished our win, we are hitting our mission. And in *Simple Church*, Thom Rainer illustrates the importance of a *simple process* for reaching and maturing people. His research of more than 400 growing and vibrant churches shows that congregations with a simple process are effective despite differences in their styles of ministry. Finally, perhaps the words of Pastor Larry Osborne of North Coast Church in Vista, California best summarizes this shift in attitude: "A church needs to decide what is its *hub* [key ministry focus], and ruthlessly guard against anything that detracts or competes with it."

Do you remember the acronym, KISS? Keep It Simple Stupid! OK, perhaps we could drop the last letter and still communicate the message. Nevertheless, as leaders of congregations and parachurch organizations, it rests on us to determine which, and how many, plates our ministry will keep spinning. The fewer and more important plates that we spin, the more productive will be our efforts.

Group Exercise:

What is your ministry win? Take a few moments to discuss what might be distracting or diluting your efforts toward accomplishing the win.

Team Prayer:

Jesus, You have told us to come unto You, and You will give us rest. Yet we confess that too often we don't feel very rested. As a leadership team we want to be sensitive to how You want us to focus our service. Keep us from a bandwagon approach of just doing what other ministries are doing, and release us from the feelings that we have to offer a program for every expressed need out there. Please give us clear direction on how to best accomplish the great commandment and great commission in this specific mission field to which You have called us. Amen!

Final Thought:

Less is more!

Success

After the death of Moses the servant of the LORD, the LORD said to Joshua son of Nun, Moses' aide: 'Moses My servant is dead. Now then, you and all these people, get ready to cross the Jordan River into the land I am about to give to them— to the Israelites. I will give you every place where you set your foot, as I promised Moses. Your territory will extend from the desert to Lebanon, and from the great river, the Euphrates— all the Hittite country— to the Mediterranean Sea in the west. No one will be able to stand against you all the days of your life. As I was with Moses, so I will be with you; I will never leave you nor forsake you. Be strong and courageous, because you will lead these people to inherit the land I swore to their ancestors to give them. Be strong and very courageous. Be careful to obey all the law My servant Moses gave you; do not turn from it to the right or to the left, that you may be successful wherever you go. Keep this Book

of the Law always on your lips; meditate on it
day and night, so that you may be careful to do
everything written in it. Then
you will be prosperous and successful. Have
I not commanded you? Be strong and
courageous. Do not be afraid; do not be
discouraged, for the LORD your God will be
with you wherever you go.'

— Joshua 1:1-9

TWO KEYNOTE SPEAKERS WERE INVITED to a national religious conference on leadership. Ironically, both men chose to speak on the subject of success.

In no uncertain terms the first speaker denounced the concept of success as a worldly philosophy that Christians should avoid. His emphasis was that God does not want us to be successful. He wants us to be faithful.

Immediately following that address, the next speaker spoke about the need for Christians to be successful. In fact, he used the word SUCCESS as an acrostic for the outline of his speech.

Needless to say, it was one of those awkward situations where the audience sympathized with the speakers, especially the second one. Although I don't remember much of the content of the speeches, it provided a great opportunity to struggle with the concept of success and its relationship to Christians.

Whose interpretation was correct? Probably both were. Much depends on the definition of the term success. One definition is "to achieve or accomplish something planned."

People usually view success from one of three perspectives: survival, surplus or significance. In order to determine whether we achieve success as leaders we need to decide which perspective produces greatest value.

Survival. In a day and age when violence, disease and disasters are rampant throughout the world, many people consider themselves successful if they make it through the day. If they are alive, and those they love are still alive, they are successful.

Surplus. When materialism is a predominant mindset, the accumulation of things becomes more than an option; it is the goal. How much a person possesses becomes the top priority. The bottom line each day revolves around multiplying wealth and one's net worth.

Significance. For those with this perspective, it is not the value of one's estate, but the significance of one's legacy that ultimately matters. Am I making a contribution in the arenas of life where God has placed me: home, church, community, school and employment? Making a difference for Christ and His Kingdom becomes the measuring stick.

A biblical view of success "is the achieving of the goals that God has helped me set." One outstanding example of a successful person was Joshua. He was not successful because he survived many battles or accumulated many possessions; he was successful because he made a Kingdom difference. In Joshua 1:8 we learn that the basis of his success was obedience to the Word of God. While Joshua was successful looking at his life from the first two perspectives, it is because of his success from the third perspective, *significance*, that his life became a role model for millennia.

So cast a long shadow; leave a rich legacy. Individually, and as a team, use your gifts and time in faithful service, and you will be successful in the eyes of God.

Group Exercise:

In a circle response, answer the question: After you are gone, how would you like people to remember you?

Team Prayer:

Victorious Lord, grant us success in completing our tasks and achieving the goals You have helped us set. Give us a Kingdom perspective. We want to make a difference in the lives of Your Church, this community and Your world. Amen!

Final Thought:

I would rather fail in a cause that will ultimately succeed, than succeed in a cause that will ultimately fail.

— Woodrow Wilson

Tension

In those days when the number of disciples was increasing, the Hellenistic Jews among them complained against the Hebraic Jews because their widows were being overlooked in the daily distribution of food. So the Twelve gathered all the disciples together and said, 'It would not be right for us to neglect the ministry of the word of God in order to wait on tables. Brothers and sisters, choose seven men from among you who are known to be full of the Spirit and wisdom. We will turn this responsibility over to them and will give our attention to prayer and the ministry of the word.' This proposal pleased the whole group. They chose Stephen, a man full of faith and of the Holy Spirit; also Philip, Procorus, Nicanor, Timon, Parmenas, and Nicolas from Antioch, a convert to Judaism. They presented them to the apostles, who prayed and laid their hands on them. So the word of God spread. The number of disciples in Jerusalem increased *rapidly, and a large number of priests became obedient to the faith.*

— Acts 6:1–7

MANY PEOPLE THINK IT WOULD be great to be a member of a ministry that never experiences tension. But would that truly be great? A young pastor in the Midwest once wrote about a 75-year-old church he was serving. "We have no tension in our church; the church is comatose. We are about dead." Within six months the pastor's fears were realized. The church without tension had died!

Some people idealize New Testament churches as being assemblies without problems. However, a careful reading of the Book of Acts reveals that each Christian community faced specific challenges. One may deny, trivialize or spiritualize the tensions, but they were very real.

In the sixth chapter of Acts, for example, Luke describes a complaint that the Grecian Jews had with the Hebraic Jews over the distribution of food. It is not apparent whether the difficulty arose because of prejudice, neglect or the heavy workload of leadership. Nevertheless, the Grecian Jews felt an inequity in the church's care giving.

Notice that the apostles did not avoid the issue or blame the participants in the controversy. Instead, they addressed their concern in a positive way. The Twelve called a meeting to discuss the matter with all the disciples, and then chose a group of seven reputable leaders to look into the problem (worthy of note, all seven were Grecian). Next the apostles prayed for and commissioned these new leaders. Then this new group assumed responsibility for the food relief, while the apostles concentrated on prayer and the ministry of the Word. Interestingly, the governance structure that many churches follow today originated from this point of tension in the early Church.

What might have happened if the Jerusalem church avoided or trivialized the tension? Most likely a greater division would have occurred. But rather than letting this issue cause division, its resolve resulted in the growth of the church, both in maturity and in outreach.

A good definition of tension is "the stretching of two opposite forces while searching for a proper balance." Consider the positive value of tension. Without it a sewing machine wouldn't function properly. Without it the bow hunter couldn't shoot an arrow. Whether it is an exercise bike or a fishing rod, without good tension a positive outcome can't happen. Likewise, without tension, in life or in an organization, we would become comatose.

Tension in ministry is inevitable. Whenever two or more people live together, differing opinions will surface. But these tensions can be viewed more positively. For we can use them to help clarify issues before us, which in turn can guide us to better achieving our purposes. So adjust your tensions as you work together as leaders. Be forthright; don't ignore them. A healthy balance will move you forward.

Group Exercise:

Identify a good tension in your present ministry.

Identify a tension that needs to move toward healthier balance.

Team Prayer:

Lord, we want peace in the church. However, as we discuss items and strategize for solutions to problems, we find ourselves in the midst of tensions. Give us discernment as to how we can use these tensions for Your Kingdom's growth. Amen!

Final Thought:

You will never be the person you can be if pressure, tension and discipline are taken out of your life.
— James G. Bilkey

Power to Lead

If you love me, keep my commands. And I will ask the Father, and he will give you another advocate to help you and be with you forever— the Spirit of Truth. The world cannot accept him, because it neither sees him nor knows him. But you know him, for he lives with you and will be in you. I will not leave you as orphans; I will come to you. But the Advocate, the Holy Spirit, whom the Father will send in my name, will teach you all things and will remind you of everything I have said to you.

— John 14:15–18, 26

WHO IS THE MOST POWERFUL person you know? Who is the most powerful person in your organization? Who is the most powerful person in the whole world? Mistakenly, too often we look at the human level for the answer, when in fact the most powerful person in all of life is the Holy Spirit.

Unfortunately, we are so accustomed to our physical world of touch, sight, sound, smell and taste that we lose sight of the noncorporeal realm around us. We weave in and out of physical traffic, eat a physical burger, stub a physical toe, and retire in a physical bed. Too easily we forget that we are loved by a heavenly Father (1 John 3:1), prayed for by a risen Savior (Hebrews 7:25) and guided by an indwelling Spirit (John 16:26).

The Holy Spirit is the one who:

- Convicts us of sin (John 16:6)
- Draws us to Christ (John 6:44)
- Brings us into the Body of Christ (1 Corinthians 12:13)
- Lives within us (Romans 8:9)
- Produces spiritual fruit in our lives (Galatians 5:22, 23)
- Leads us (Romans 8:14)
- Assures us (Romans 8:16)
- Intercedes for us (Romans 8:26)
- Restrains evil (2 Thessalonians 2:7)
- Gives us discernment (1 Corinthians 2:10)
- Teaches us (John 16:13)
- Influences us (Ephesians 5:18)
- Gives us joy and peace (Romans 14:17)
- Gives us ministry gifts (1 Corinthians 12:11)
- Seals us securely in Christ (Ephesians 1:13, 14)

Now this is great news! God has given each Christian this divine *Helper*. He has placed within us His resident *Truth*

Teacher. You cannot be a believer and not have the Holy Spirit: "And if anyone does not have the Spirit of Christ, they do not belong to Christ" (Romans 8:9b). God leads us through His Word by the guiding of His Spirit.

However, the purpose for the Spirit's divine power in our lives goes far beyond our personal well being. The omnipotent Holy Spirit resides in us for another reason. In the words of Jesus: "But you will receive power when the Holy Spirit comes upon you; you will be my witnesses in Jerusalem, and in all Judea and Samaria, and to the ends of the earth" (Acts 1:8). Christ's plan is to reach all people groups through Spirit-empowered believers.

As Christ followers God desires transformation in our lives and in our churches. And this transformation deepens every time we say *yes* to the Spirit. His power is unleashed in and through devoted lives.

As a ministry team pray that God's Spirit will guide you. When you get worried by pressures, or discouraged by problems, reflect on the reality of God's Spirit within you. And always take confidence that, by His Spirit, "He who began a good work in you will carry it on to completion until the day of Christ Jesus" (Philippians 1:6).

Group Exercise:

Take a moment and share your response to one of the following questions:
1. What is one way you can use the Helper's help right now?

2. What scriptural truth does the Truth Teacher need to ingrain more deeply into your mind?

Team Prayer:

Thank You, Lord, for giving us the Holy Spirit. Thank You for providing such a complete salvation. And thank You for the diversity of gifts that Your Spirit has given to those in this room. Help us as a board to follow the leading of the Spirit, as we joyfully work in Your harvest. This we ask in the strong name of Jesus. Amen!

Final Thought:

You will always win when playing Follow the Leader, if the Leader you follow is the Holy Spirit!

Competition

For since there is jealousy and quarreling among you, are you not worldly? Are you not acting like mere human beings? For when one says, 'I follow Paul,' and another, 'I follow Apollos,' are you not mere human beings? What, after all, is Apollos? And what is Paul? Only servants, through whom you came to believe— as the Lord has assigned to each his task. I planted the seed, Apollos watered it, but God has been making it grow. So neither the one who plants nor the one who waters is anything, but only God, who makes things grow. The one who plants and the one who waters have one purpose, and they will each be rewarded according to their own labor. For we are God's co-workers; you are God's field, God's building.

— 1 Corinthians 3:3–9

A FARMER PLACED AN OSTRICH egg in his chicken coop. Someone asked if he was expecting the hens to produce ostrich eggs. "No," he replied. "I just want them to understand what the competition is like!" Unfortunately, competition not only surfaces in the chicken coop, in the classroom and on the playing field, but it can also surface in Christian ministry.

We live in a highly competitive society. Most people work at tasks that constantly remind them that they are in competition with other companies, and at times with one another.

Some people assume that Christian ministries should function like a business. And while the church and parachurch organizations must have business-like characteristics such as goals, purposes and accountability, they are more than a mere organization. They are also an organism. Jesus is the head, and the members of the Church are the body.

The neuro-muscular design of the body lets it function with phenomenal symbiotic cooperation. In a similar way, the Church, the Body of Christ, is also designed with complementary parts. Unfortunately, in some situations like in the church at Corinth, leaders are compared in a competitive way. The Corinthians were reflecting a worldly perspective. Some were following Paul and some were following Apollos. They needed to be reminded that Christ is the head of the Church, and that they should avoid comparing one leader to another. Both Paul and Apollos were simply workers in the harvest.

Program teams are also vulnerable to the pressures of comparison and competition. Competition can arise over the recruitment of volunteers to various ministries. It can also surface over budget needs and the allocation of resources.

Confusion about authority and decision making can lead to strife or power struggles. For example, many churches are unclear on what the pastor(s) may decide, what committees may decide and what should be voted on by the congregation as a whole. Misunderstandings in the area of authority and decision making have hurt many churches.

On a more personal side, individuals serving on a ministry team bring with them their own personalities, philosophies, priorities and perspectives. The potential for disagreement or competition among team leaders is always present.

Therefore, it's important to periodically remind ourselves whose side we are on. Ultimately, we are all on the side of Christ. We are all committed to building His Church. Recall that it was Jesus Himself who reminded His disciples: "Whoever is not against you is for you" (Luke 9:50b).

As members of a ministry team we are not in competition with one another or with other ministry teams. "We" and "they" conversations should never occur. We are they! We are all on the same team, and therefore need to push past any type of comparison. By keeping our eyes on Christ, we can avoid the self-focused tendency of competition.

Group Exercise:

How competitive is your ministry environment? To what degree is there comparison among programs or with other groups? Take a moment to pray for your ministry's closest competitor. After all, they are really your partner.

Team Prayer:

Lord, guard us from the sense of comparison and competition. Help us to remember that this is not our ministry, but Yours. When You are in control, we are all winners. May our efforts always be centered in Jesus Christ and His Kingdom.
Amen!

Final Thought:

The higher the stakes, the greater the possibility of losing your temper over the game.

— C.S. Lewis

Uncertainty

During the night the mystery was revealed to Daniel in a vision. Then Daniel praised the God of heaven and said: 'Praise be to the name of God for ever and ever; wisdom and power are his. He changes times and seasons; he deposes kings and raises up others. He gives wisdom to the wise and knowledge to the discerning. He reveals deep and hidden things; he knows what lies in darkness, and light dwells with him. I thank and praise You, God of my ancestors: You have given me wisdom and power, you have made known to me what we asked of You, You have made known to us the dream of the king.' Then Daniel went to Arioch, whom the king had appointed to execute the wise men of Babylon, and said to him, 'Do not execute the wise men of Babylon. Take me to the king, and I will interpret his dream for him.' Arioch took Daniel to the king at once and said, 'I have found a man among the exiles from Judah who can tell

> the king what his dream means.' The king asked
> Daniel (also called Belteshazzar), 'Are you able
> to tell me what I saw in my dream and interpret
> it?' Daniel replied, 'No wise man, enchanter,
> magician or diviner can explain to the king the
> mystery he has asked about, but there is a God
> in heaven who reveals mysteries. He has shown
> King Nebuchadnezzar what will happen in days
> to come. Your dream and the visions that passed
> through your mind as you were lying in bed are
> these. . .'
>
> — Daniel 2:19–28

"DO YOU KNOW WHAT YOU are getting into?" People have been asked that question many times, especially when changing jobs or moving to a new location. Wouldn't it be helpful to know ahead of time what situations you have to face before you encounter them? Or would it?

After years of living with the uncertainties of life and ministry, I've [Fred] come to the conclusion that I am thankful I didn't always know what I was getting into. The bottom line is, in some situations had I known what I was getting into, I probably would have been too discouraged to do anything.

In the Bible narrative above, Daniel and his three friends lived with uncertainty. They dwelt in a foreign land, with a different culture, another language and a godless value system. Falsely accused, they were sentenced to death. In the midst of the uncertainty of life, Daniel responded positively and prayed to God in confidence, believing that his God could even rearrange governments (Daniel 2:21).

A negative response to uncertainty is recorded in Mark's gospel. When Jesus arrived in the region of the Gerasenes, He encountered a demon-possessed man, cast the demons out of him and sent them into a heard of pigs feeding on the nearby hillside (see Mark 5:1–20). When the townsfolk saw the man "sitting there, dressed and in his right mind," and learned that their pigs had rushed down a steep bank into the lake and were drowned, "they were afraid." One of the saddest verses in Scripture records that the townsfolk began to "plead with Jesus to leave their region" (v. 17). Their fear of the unknown kept them from embracing the power of God. What a contrast to Daniel's uncertainty that moved him and his friends to accept the power of God.

One of the greatest gifts God gives to His children is the blessing of uncertainty. The Apostle Paul gave us these words to help focus our trust: "Command those who are rich in this present world not to be arrogant nor to put their hope in wealth, which is so uncertain, but to put their hope in God, who richly provides us with everything for our enjoyment" (1 Timothy 6:17).

As leaders you recognize that planning is important. And in many situations, predictability is possible. But Christian ministry has its moments of uncertainty. In those times, we can rest in the certainty of God's presence with us. His knowledge, grace, and power always surround us.

Group Exercise:

In pairs, take a brief moment and share one area in which you are experiencing uncertainty. Pray for God's direction and peace for one another.

Team Prayer:

Sovereign Lord, thank You for Your control in the life of this ministry. We confess that sometimes the obstacles we face appear to be overwhelming. Help us learn to trust You with the present as well as the future. This is Your work. May we be faithful stewards of all You have entrusted. Amen!

Final Thought:

We don't know what the future holds, but we know who holds the future!

Remember

When you have eaten and are satisfied, praise the
LORD your God for the good land he has given
you. Be careful that you do not forget the LORD
your God, failing to observe his commands, his
laws and his decrees that I am giving you this
day. Otherwise, when you eat and are satisfied,
when you build fine houses and settle down,
and when your herds and flocks grow large and
your silver and gold increase and all you have
is multiplied, then your heart will become proud
and you will forget the LORD your God, who
brought you out of Egypt, out of the land of
slavery.

— Deuteronomy 8:10–14

NO DOUBT, SOMEONE YOU KNOW has a poor memory. There are
jokes about absent-minded professors, forgetful husbands and
aging seniors. But whether it's a case of amnesia or Alzheimer's,
serious memory loss is no joking matter. And in light of eternity,
perhaps even more tragic is spiritual dementia.

In the historical passage above, Moses reminds the Israelites to *remember* how the Lord, their God, delivered them from Egypt and guided them through the wilderness. He further admonishes them not to *forget* the Lord when they gain prosperity in the land of promise. For many, it's easy to remember the Lord in times of trouble. Instinctively we cry out for His help. In this passage, God's people are challenged to also remember the Lord in times of abundance and satisfaction. A good memory keeps us honest, humble and honoring of God.

In the New Testament we find similar exhortations to remember. Peter, for example, encouraged Christians to develop a number of character qualities: "faith, goodness, knowledge, self-control, perseverance, godliness, mutual affection, and love" (2 Peter 1:5–7). We can easily concur with the apostle that these qualities will keep us from being "ineffective and unproductive" in our relationship with Christ (v. 8).

But the key verse in that passage may be verse 9, which states: "but if anyone does not have them, they are nearsighted and blind, and they have forgotten that they have been cleansed from their past sins." Did you see it? Sure, we are to desire the great character qualities mentioned above. But if they are slipping in our lives, there's one explanation—it's because of memory loss. When we remember our past and God's gracious forgiveness, we're motivated to live a Christ-honoring life.

In the letters to the seven churches, Jesus also addressed the theme of remembering. After commending the church in Ephesus for their perseverance, hard work and orthodoxy (Revelation 2:1–3), He criticized them for forsaking their first love (v. 4). Christ's recommended cure for their lost passion was to "remember the height from which you have fallen! Repent and do the things you did at first" (v. 5a).

In spite of being surrounded by a hostile spiritual culture, this church was heavily engaged in ministry. But somehow in the process of Kingdom service, they allowed their relationship with the King to cool. So Jesus reminded them to get back to the basics of the intimate communion they had with Him at the beginning of their relationship.

Remembering is so critical to our spiritual journey that our Lord gave His followers an object lesson to perpetually jog our memories. On the night before He gave His life for us, Jesus took bread, gave thanks and broke it and gave it to His disciples saying, "This is My body given for you; do this in remembrance of Me'" (Luke 22:19).

The communion service reminds us that we were separated from God; that the penalty for our sin was death; and that Jesus Christ paid our penalty. And as Paul emphasizes: "For whenever you eat this bread and drink this cup, you proclaim the Lord's death until He comes" (1 Corinthians 11:26). The Lord's Supper is an ongoing reminder of God's mercy.

As leaders, let's be diligent in service. But more importantly, let's always remember the One we serve in ministry. And if any words of praise come our way, may we be even more appreciative that the Lord has invited us to share in His harvest.

Group Exercise:

Reflect back on a time of special closeness to God.

What contributed to this intimacy?

Team Prayer:

Father, we know the dark side of our lives.
Therefore we are deeply appreciative of Your love
and mercy. We do not serve in an attempt to
earn Your favor, but to humbly let others know of
Your goodness and provision in Christ. You have
ordained that we be born in this particular place
and at this particular time. Keep our memories of
Your mercy fresh on our minds, and we will serve
You with deep gratitude. Amen!

Final Thought:

Forget tying a bow on your finger; instead,
meditate on God's mercies each day!

Using What You Have

Then the LORD said to him, 'What is that in
your hand?' 'A staff,' he replied. The LORD
said, 'Throw it on the ground.' Moses threw it on
the ground and it became a snake, and he ran
from it. Then the LORD said to him, 'Reach
out your hand and take it by the tail.' So Moses
reached out and took hold of the snake and it
turned back into a staff in his hand. 'This,'
said the LORD, 'is so that they may believe that
the LORD, the God of their fathers— the God of
Abraham, the God of Isaac and the God of Jacob—
has appeared to you.'
— Exodus 4:2–5

I [JOHN] DON'T KNOW ABOUT you, but I'd have to be real sure
that it was God speaking before I'd pick up a snake by its tail. If
forced to grab one, everyone knows you should grab it behind
the head. But God was demonstrating to Moses (and to all of us

through this account) that His power can be manifested even through the common things in our lives. The staff of Moses became the rod of God, and was used in miraculous ways on behalf of God's people.

Reviewing other biblical narratives we also observe how God used:

- A slingshot in the hand of David to free the Israelites (1 Samuel 17)

- An ox goad in the hand of Shamgar to deter God's enemies (Judges 3:31)

- A handful of flour and a few ounces of oil in the hand of a widow to sustain a prophet and feed her family for years (1 Kings 17:7–24)

- Two fish and five rolls from a boy to feed more than five thousand people (John 6:1–15)

- A boat from a fisherman to transport Christ from village to village (Mark 8:10)

- A staff in the hand of Dorcus to clothe friends (Acts 9:36–41)

- The private tomb of Joseph to temporarily house the Son of Man (Mark 15:42–47)

The details and blessings of each of these accounts are worth a full read. But for now it's easy to simply affirm that God can use anything we yield to Him for service.

As leaders you have likely completed personality profiles or leadership style inventories. You recognize that God works through your distinct wiring. As teammates you likely have job descriptions that specify service expectations, and God also uses these focused acts of service.

But think for a moment about service possibilities beyond gifting, competencies and job expectations. Look at the mundane. Reflect on the more common. What are some small actions that can be a blessing to others?

On any given day it might not be the meeting itself, but giving somebody a ride to the meeting that will make deeper impact. Maybe it's not the role we play on the team, but the hug for a hurting teammate that will matter the most. And perhaps it's not the visibility from the platform that casts as long a shadow as the time behind the scenes coaching a younger leader.

When God asks you: "What is that in your hand?" What might you answer?

Group Exercise:

Identify a personal possession that can be used by God to bless others.

Team Prayer:

Dear Jesus, we know You told the apostle Paul that Your power is made perfect in weakness. So use the little things in our lives, the mustard seeds, the small talents and modest possessions to bring You glory. Together as a team, and individually as Your followers, use the small things in our lives to touch others and bring You much praise. Amen!

Final Thought:

A little becomes a lot when placed in the hands of God!

Keeping the Big Picture!

Therefore, I urge you, brothers and sisters, in view of God's mercy, to offer your bodies as a living sacrifice, holy and pleasing to God— this is true worship. Do not conform to the pattern of this world, but be transformed by the renewing of your mind. Then you will be able to test and approve what God's will is— his good, pleasing and perfect will.

— Romans 12:1–2

OFTEN IN MINISTRY WE ARE deeply involved in program planning and execution. We move from meeting to meeting, and event to event. The loop never closes. Pull off a great program, for example, and the deadline for the next one is just six days away. Yes, "go and make disciples" is a command, but so is "Be still and know that I am God."

It is important, therefore, to periodically step back and reflect on the big picture. This study passage reminds us first and foremost that we are God's children, and our deepest pleasure is found in spiritual transformation. So let me [John] put the work of your ministry team in proper perspective by offering the following reminders:

You are honoring Christ, more than serving on a ministry team. The above text states that your commitment is holy and pleasing to God. Few people get excited about serving on another task group. But it is exciting to think you can bring pleasure to God through joyful service. Paul admonished: "Whatever you do, work at it with all your heart as working for the Lord, not people" (Colossians 3:23). To the church at Corinth he emphasized: "So whatever you eat or drink or whatever you do, do it all for the glory of God" (1 Cor. 10:31).

You are worshiping, more than working. Interestingly, some Bible scholars translate the Greek expression in verse one as "your spiritual worship," while others translate it "your reasonable service." The Greek word used there, *latreia*, may be translated worship, service or ministry. Many people have a limited understanding of worship—they think it is what happens in an auditorium on a Sunday morning. But the Bible teaches that daily living should be an act of worship. As members of a ministry team you are doing far more than planning events and working in a program. You are, in essence, worshiping through these activities.

You are choosing encounters of significance more than escapades of escape. While many activities in our daily schedules are prescribed because of responsibilities at work or with family, everyone has some discretionary time. Certainly participating in an athletic activity, attending the theater or even watching TV can serve as a relaxing break. But some people seem to weary themselves in pursuit of amusement and pleasure. Life requires that the grass be mowed, groceries be purchased, and clothes be laundered. But at the end of each week, if only work, chores and leisure activities define life, then the urgent was probably placed ahead of the important. The Bible affirms: "Be very careful how you live— not as unwise but as wise, making the most of every opportunity...." (Ephesians 5:15, 16a). Although serving on a ministry team takes a big chunk out of your schedule, remember that your time invested here will pay eternal dividends.

You are doing what is natural, not exceptional. Because you are a member of a ministry team, I commend you for your commitment to Christ and His church. However, at the same time please realize that serving Christ is natural for His followers. Some people think that only the specially gifted or spiritually mature can serve. However, this passage affirms that worshipful service is a natural, reasonable act. It flows automatically from being devoted to Jesus. Christian service is not for the exceptional few. For the believer it should be as natural as breathing. It is a call for all Christ followers, as they routinely inhale God's goodness and exhale His fruit onto others through service.

You are fulfilling a spiritual calling, not filling a ministry slot. If by serving we are doing what is natural because God has pre-wired us for good works, then it is through exercising our spiritual gifts and abilities that we find true fulfillment. When Christian service is viewed as filling a ministry slot, joy is rarely the result. In the verses that follow this text (vv. 3–8), Paul delineates the gifts of preaching, helping, teaching, encouraging, contributing, leading and showing mercy. These gifts, however, will only produce fruit with resulting fulfillment when they are planted in the field of service.

Group Exercise:

Which of the above contrasts is most insightful or relevant to you right now? Why?

Team Prayer:

Father, we realize that the work of our ministry team is important; we do not take our service in Christ's Church lightly. We ask that You continue to deepen our appreciation for the value of Kingdom service. Open our eyes and hearts to see our ministry as an act of worship pleasing to You. Amen!

Final Thought:

Some workers view their job as laying bricks; others see the task as building a cathedral. Embrace the bigger picture!

Made in the USA